PRA
HOW TO
YOUR CHURCH

Ralph Moore shares his lifetime of experience in multiplying churches and his insights into what God is doing around the world in sparking church-planting movements. I read this book in one sitting. Ralph has a way of drawing you in, winning you over and pointing the way forward in multiplying disciples, leaders and churches.

Steve Addison

Director of Church Resource Ministries, Australia
Author, *Movements That Change the World*

There are very few people in America qualified to write a book about multiplying churches. Ralph Moore is one of the few. While others grow Godzilla-sized churches, Ralph quietly sets out to multiply and release leaders and churches to the ends of the earth. For that reason, he is one of my heroes.

Neil Cole

Founder and Director, Church Multiplication Associates
Author, *Organic Church*, *Organic Leadership* and *Search and Rescue*

This book will inspire you with Ralph Moore's heartbeat for church planting, but more importantly with God's desire to multiply churches around the world. This is a book about vision and hope for reaching a world for Jesus Christ. You will be stirred to believe in God-shaped possibilities for multiplying congregations and even church-planting movements. You will find practical, down-to-earth advice written in a winsome, engaging way. You'll love this book, just like I did.

Joel Comiskey, Ph.D.

Founder, Joel Comiskey Group
Author, *Planting Churches That Reproduce*

There is hardly any church of any type, denomination or size that could not learn from this book. Through examples from his own experience and clear application of biblical principles, Ralph leads us back to the future. The answers are not in sterile models and methods but rather in dynamic movements. As he so eloquently describes it, the New Testament Church is not the "primitive Church" but the "prototype."

Tony and Felicity Dale
Founders, The Karis Group
Authors, *The Rabbit and the Elephant*

Ralph Moore again demonstrates why he is one of the leading voices in the missional movement. *How to Multiply Your Church* addresses a key oversight in many of the church-planting conversations: the multiplication strategy of the church. This book could become a standard for students, church planters, pastors and leaders who believe God can radically change the landscape of our world through His Church.

Dr. Rodney A. Harrison
Director of Doctoral Studies, Midwestern Baptist Theological Seminary
Author, *Seven Steps to Church Planting* and *Spin-off Churches*

The practical wisdom and no-nonsense frankness of Ralph Moore's leadership style shines throughout this book. He is a twenty-first century church planter who has found how to lead with a mindset and capability consistent with the Holy Spirit's tactics in the New Testament. I know no more effective current model as a pastoral advocate for and dynamic practitioner of church planting than him.

Jack W. Hayford
Chancellor, The King's Seminary

Ralph is one of the premier practitioners of church planting in the English-speaking world. You will be encouraged by this book, which takes the unnecessary complexity out of the process and adds fun and excitement to your Kingdom expansion adventure.

David Housholder
Church Planter, Robinwood Church of Huntington Beach, California
Author, *Light Your Church on Fire Without Burning It Down*

Few practitioners could have written on this subject with such clarity, putting the dream of reproduction within reach of every pastor who dares nurture the thought. Ralph gently but firmly makes the case that health ought to lead to reproduction. This book is brilliant in its simplicity. It is not a call to strategy or tactics but an invitation to faith and action. Though intensely personal, the fate of thousands rests on this decision: "Will I allow the church I pastor to multiply?" Ralph Moore dismantles our objections and gives us every reason to say yes.

Rod Koop
Facilitator, Foursquare Church Multiplication

Packing decades of experience into one unique wallop, Ralph Moore stretches the boundaries of church-growth thinking through the genius of brilliant and simple innovations set forth in a refreshing "can do" spirit. Learn how your church, no matter what size, can seize divine momentum and sustain exponential multi-generational impact.

Norman Nakanishi
Senior Pastor, Grace Bible Church, Pearl City, Hawaii
U.S. National Leadership Team, Every Nation Family of Churches

Ralph Moore has written an intriguing book to tell us how to multiply a church in the most effective way. He was a student of mine in the 1970s and we have been friends for the past 30 years, and now he has written a book to point us toward the Great Commission—to "go and make disciples of all nations." May God use this book to strengthen churches everywhere.

Elmer L. Towns
Cofounder, Liberty University

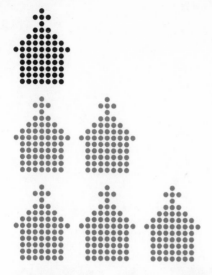

HOW TO **MULTIPLY** YOUR CHURCH

The Most Effective Way to Grow

RALPH MOORE

Author of *Starting a New Church* and Founder of the Hope Chapel Movement

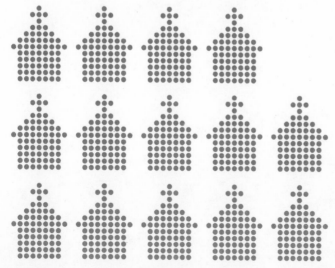

Regal

From Gospel Light
Ventura, California, U.S.A.

Published by Regal
From Gospel Light
Ventura, California, U.S.A.
www.regalbooks.com
Printed in the U.S.A.

Library of Congress Cataloging-in-Publication Data
Moore, Ralph, 1945-
How to multiply your church : the most effective way to grow / Ralph Moore.
p. cm.
Includes bibliographical references.
ISBN 978-0-8307-5133-4 (trade paper)
1. Church growth. I. Title.
BV652.25.M65 2009
254—dc22
2009013212

1 2 3 4 5 6 7 8 9 10 11 12 13 14 15 / 15 14 13 12 11 10 09

Rights for publishing this book outside the U.S.A. or in non-English languages are
administered by Gospel Light Worldwide, an international not-for-profit ministry.
For additional information, please visit www.glww.org, email info@glww.org, or
write to Gospel Light Worldwide, 1957 Eastman Avenue, Ventura, CA 93003, U.S.A.

CONTENTS

Part 3: In Search of Scripture

Part 4: Opportunity Is Where You Make It

Part 5: You *Can* Do This!

Part 6: Stand and Deliver

FOREWORD

Multiplication changes things. In one of the classic episodes of that cultural phenomenon called *Star Trek*, the crew of the Enterprise encountered some lovable little fuzzballs called Tribbles. The crew fell in love with these cute little creatures—that is, until they overwhelmed the vessel through rapid multiplication. Tribbles multiplied faster than rabbits. Multiplication changes things.

In *How to Multiply Your Church*, Ralph Moore points out clearly and poignantly that the North American Church has some church-planting "trouble with tribbles." We need to abandon our addiction to church-as-usual and fall in love with multiplication. Ralph brings us into the light of a new reproductive church paradigm. Churches in North America desperately need Ralph's message and practical experience. Hopefully, this work will help spark a movement.

Ralph's book is rich in historical insight, filled with biblical acumen, and applicable to the current realities of church planting. His discussion of fourth-generation disciple making, saturation church planting, benefits of multiplying and New Testament models are invaluable. His book is practical, challenging and insightful. Leaders who hunger for reaching another level of ministry impact will want to read and apply the principles found in *How to Multiply Your Church*.

Ralph observes that because churches and pastors count individual converts, they have a hard time advancing from an addition mentality. Think about it this way: When children learn their *ABC*s and how to count, it's exciting for parents. Then children learn how to combine letters to make words and learn how to add and subtract numbers—which can be a frustrating time for children and parents. Both can wonder if all the sounding out of words and counting is really going to lead anywhere. Maybe that's why so many churches and pastors never move on to multiplication—it's difficult. Multiplication is even more difficult to do once it is embraced. And it's hard to figure out how to do it. Simple addition is easier.

But most people don't stop with learning their *ABC*s or how to add and subtract. Somewhere in the middle of sounding out words and counting, something happens. Words explode into phrases, sentences, paragraphs, books and writing. Numbers explode into the world of multiplication and division. When that happens, a new world begins to take shape for children and parents.

For too long, the Church in North America has been stuck in the comfortable *ABC*s and simple counting phase of Church. We do not have to stay there. Don't get me wrong—I am not against practicing our *ABC*s (practicing basic spiritual disciplines) and counting things (measuring who we reach). But God wants us to build on that foundation and let Him take things to a new world—a world where disciples and churches are multiplying. That new world, as Ralph Moore points out, will require changing the way we think about and do church. An attitude of increase will be required.

So, what will this new world of multiplication look like? What will it take to change churches from addition to multiplication and then from multiplication to rapid multiplication or movement? First, we must get ourselves, our egos and our puny ideas out of the way. Second, we must ask God to increase in our lives and our churches. We must ask God for . . .

1. **Bigger faith.** When was the last time you asked God to do something in your life or in the life of your church that made His name and His fame great?

That's what the disciples asked of Jesus: "Increase our faith!" (Luke 17:5, *NIV*). For some, just asking them to think about reproduction and multiplication is like asking them to think about trying extreme skiing, much less actually having them doing anything about it. We need to ask for bigger faith. The new question is, "What does God want?"

2. Greater focus on Jesus. John the Baptizer said, "He must increase, but I must decrease" (John 3:30, *NASB*). Think about it: John had a pretty good thing going. I mean, aside from a weird diet and slightly unfashionable dress. He had all these people coming to him, he had his own followers, and he got to put the smackdown on the religious leaders. What a gig! But once Jesus arrived on the scene, John pointed people solely in His direction. John even encouraged those following him to follow Jesus. John and John's kingdom were no longer the issue—Jesus and His kingdom were. The new question is, "Who is this all about?"

3. *Fresh boldness in sharing His Word.* This happened throughout the book of Acts. In fact, at one point Luke reported, "But the word of God continued to increase and spread" (Acts 12:24, *NIV*). When Paul was in prison, he asked the church at Ephesus to pray that he would share God's message with boldness. The Word of God is increasing, and it is spreading in other parts of the world right now. So the new question is, "Why not again in North America?"

4. Overflowing and expanding love. Multiplying disciples and churches requires a special kind of love for Jesus, His Church and the lost peoples around the world. Paul prayed that the church at Thessalonica would direct God's love to those in their world. I like the way *THE MESSAGE* words it: "And may the Master pour on the love so it fills your lives and splashes over on everyone around you, just as it does from us to you. May you be infused with strength and purity, filled with confidence in the presence of God our Father when our Master Jesus arrives with all his followers" (1 Thess. 3:12-13). The new question is, "How are you praying?"

In its recent history, the Church Growth Movement in North America has been more about a Grow *My* Church Movement. What Ralph describes so well in this book is that we need a Disciples Multiplying Churches Movement. If God would graciously give us a fresh outpouring of each of these four things described above, we might see that kind of multiplicative movement. Ralph Moore has challenged us to think about it and seek it. He has called those who are willing to step out in faith and do it.

If you believe that God is nudging you to respond to that call, this is my prayer for you: "May the LORD make you increase, both you and your children" (Ps. 115:14, *NIV*).

May *we* change so that multiplication can change even more things for God's glory in the world.

Ed Stetzer
Director of Lifeway's Research and Lifeway's Missiologist in Residence
Author, *Breaking the Missional Code* and *Comeback Churches*

INTRODUCTION

BE FRUITFUL, MULTIPLY...
AND FILL ALL THE EARTH

It's been almost a decade since Bill Greig from Regal asked me to write this book. At that time, I was focused on the need for the Church to recognize that those people identified as Generation X had needs that differed from those of the Baby Boomers. Regal graciously published a book on that subject called *Friends: Keys to Evangelizing Generation X*. Then it seemed the time had come to get on with the book you hold in your hands.

But the Christian community was still intensely focused on the needs of the Baby Boomer. Megachurches were (and are) doing a great job. Seeker-driven congregations seemed poised to carry us into a kind of heaven on earth where evangelism would sweep entire communities into relationship with Jesus Christ. Church multiplication was simply not a big deal in America. I was sure this book, if I wrote it, was destined for eBay or the discount booksellers.

So instead, I wrote *Starting a New Church*. I thought there might be a cadre of young pastors interested in starting something different from church as they knew it. It turns out there were quite a few. As my thinking went, they weren't in a position to multiply churches. That power belonged to established pastors who were just not that interested in multiplication.

Yet *Starting a New Church* still didn't satisfy the original request for a book on church multiplication. Although the publishers thought it would sell 5,000 to 6,000 copies in its lifetime, we were amazed to note that it doubled those numbers in the first year. It's still no bestseller (what church-growth book could be?), but I recently saw it in a catalog of Regal's 200 all-time bestsellers.

Seeing the church-planting book on that list signaled the time had come for a book on church multiplication. So I wrote this book, mostly for those pastors who used *Starting a New Church* as one of their tools when they planted the church they now pastor. My assumption is that people who have already made one sacrifice to reach an unreached generation are willing to make further sacrifices to reach yet another. They are willing to invest time, energy, money and their very selves into disciplemaking that results in church multiplication.

Throughout the book of Genesis, we find the words "fruitful" and "multiply." In several instances they are used together: "Be fruitful and multiply . . ." God spoke them to Adam, Noah, Abraham, Ishmael, Isaac and Jacob. He even spoke those words over the birds and the bees. Abraham was told that nations would come of his multiplying efforts. In short, God is into multiplication.

Multiplication (not addition) is what this book is all about. It is not about church growth in the conventional sense but in the parlance of the apostles, or of church-growth pioneer Donald MacGavran. It is growth through the rapid reproduction of churches. Churches like yours!

• •

An invitation: Before you begin, I'd like to invite you to watch a two-and-half minute video where I explain why I use World War II as the unifying metaphor throughout this book. You can catch the video at www.ralphmoorehawaii.com. Just look for the name of this book under the "links" section on the front page.

PART 1

TO ADD, MULTIPLY OR BOTH?

1

WHY 1943 WAS A VERY GOOD YEAR

• •

A CHURCH MULTIPLICATION METAPHOR

In the devastating horror of war that encompassed the years 1939 through 1945—a war in which every major world power became involved—the year 1943 was a good year. It was a time when free people amassed momentum against slaughterhouse dictators in both Europe and Asia and revealed a first sign that a tipping point was near.

The year before had been frightful. Evil marched to triumph in three continents.

For Americans, the horrors of 1942 began with the bombing of Pearl Harbor. Things only got worse as the year progressed. We suffered mostly defeat and loss throughout that year.

By the time we got into the European war, the Nazis had overrun every Western nation, save England, which teetered on the precipice and appeared to be doomed to fall to nightly air raids. Hitler dominated Europe and North Africa, and threatened the Middle East with its precious and strategic petroleum reserves.

The Pacific news was worse. Japanese troops controlled much of China. They soundly routed American forces in the Philippines. They beat the British in Singapore and defeated the Dutch in Indonesia. Missionaries were being expelled and dying across Asia.

A few more Axis victories could have tolled the end of democracy. The U. S. Navy was in danger of eternal rest on the bottom of the Pacific. If the tide didn't turn, the United States and Canada would soon find themselves completely isolated, because much of Latin America was cautiously siding with Hitler and the Japanese.

The world was a bad place to live from 1937 to mid-1942. But then the breeze began blowing in another direction.

Small victories bought time for the war to be won on another front—the home front. Thousands of miles from the front lines, British, Russian and American farms and factories mounted an unprecedented attack against the Axis powers.

By the end of 1943, we were winning the war in the factories, farmlands and marching fields back home. The Allies simply out-produced their adversaries in every way. They manufactured weapons, grew food and trained personnel at a rate the Axis powers found unimaginable. By the end of the year, even the shooting had begun to turn in our favor. Almost daily, from early 1943 to the surrender, we took out more enemy planes and aircraft carriers than they did ours, further tipping the balance of power.

Victory wouldn't be official until 1945. But you could say that 1943 was the year that ensured victory over the forces of hate.

A New Paradigm and a New Productivity

What had to change to advance the cause of democracy? Three things: (1) a paradigm change of thinking about the war itself; (2) the mass introduction of men and materials into the cause; and (3) a "wedding of necessity" joining Western democracies and the totalitarian Soviet Union. Lacking those ingredients the world was doomed to decades, perhaps centuries, of slavery and genocide. First, let's look at the paradigm shift.

Coming Out of Isolation

It happened almost overnight. Before the attack on Pearl Harbor, America had been spellbound by the propaganda of ignorance and isolation.

Popular wisdom held that America was safe, its continent an island of tranquility separated from war by two very large oceans. Isolationist America remained undaunted throughout the late 1930s as Germany conquered most of Europe through a vile mixture of guile and lightning war. They sat tight during 1940, while Hitler overran France and drenched London in her own blood with a nightly rain of bombs. Without a change of thinking, America would sit this one out.

Then our enemies did us two favors in a single week. First, the Japanese killed 2,200 Americans at Pearl Harbor. Four days later, Hitler and Italy's Mussolini foolishly declared war on the United States to show unity with their Asian partners.

Those were the biggest mistakes the Axis countries could have made. They awakened the sleeping giant, America. Once U. S. citizens felt threatened, they reviewed their position. Pearl Harbor and open declaration of war opened America to new and threatening possibilities. That simple paradigm change became a significant key to victory.

Production More Important Than Prowess

The second change involved a rapid acceleration of fighting power by sheer increase of manpower and weaponry. False tranquility had dug a deeper hole in the American psyche. We weren't equipped to fight. During 1939, as the world burned,

America reduced her army from 156,000 to 49,000 men.[1] Twenty years after the end of World War I, "the war to end all wars," the United States fielded only the thirteenth largest army in the world.

But the United States had the *capacity* to produce soldiers and equipment in a hurry. Barely a year after Pearl Harbor, we were fighting in North Africa and busily preparing for the invasion of Europe and the battle that would take the fight all the way to Berlin.

It's important to note that early in the war our planes were not as maneuverable or as fast as the Japanese Zero. And the Germans had better planes, tanks and heavy guns throughout the entire duration of hostilities. Even as late as the invasion of Normandy in 1944, seasoned German soldiers wrote letters home describing the poor fighting quality of the American and British soldiers, most of whom had never seen battle before D-Day.[2]

Our lack of preparation was more dangerous than it seems on the surface. During the war, Germany developed jet aircraft and medium-range ballistic missiles, two technologies the Allies only perfected after capturing German technology at war's end.[3] Had German technology proceeded at a faster clip, we would surely have lost the world to evil.

Victory came through a combination of high productivity on one side and attrition on the other. The attrition could not have happened without the great increase in productivity. We compensated for our lack of technological prowess by the sheer force of numbers.

The Allies—Great Britain, Russia, the United States (and France)—united to beat the Axis powers with often-inferior equipment and after suffering unimaginable losses at the outset of conflict. Allied forces, a collection of inexperienced citizen-soldiers, destroyed battle-hardened armies. Many American troops were farmers who had never traveled a hundred miles from home before being shipped off to fight on another continent. The Allies waged war by tsunami. They simply overwhelmed the enemy with superior numbers on every front.

Sons of the Great Depression learned to march, with broomsticks for rifles. Automotive factories became arsenals of war. Hope grew proportionately. The Allies in general and the United States in particular believed they could overwhelm their adversary with uncomplicated arms manned by personnel with merely adequate training. And their plan worked—they won.

A "Wedding of Necessity"

Our initial losses highlighted the third problem and the need for change—we were fighting, and losing, on *many* fronts while our enemies remained largely unscathed. Their supply lines were short and their captured territories could only be breached by invasion from the sea—the most difficult military maneuver of all.

England and America desperately needed to force our enemies to watch their back while we attacked their front. Both the Germans and the Japanese had the luxury of fighting where and when they chose. We needed to open a third front to occupy them while we built reserves for the primary invasion of Europe.

It would be Hitler who provided that third front when he foolishly turned on his former ally, Josef Stalin. His invasion of Stalingrad would prove itself an important element in the ultimate allied victory.

Political idealism naturally kept the Americans and British apart from Soviet Communists. However, political pragmatism forced us to realize that we needn't like each other to *need* and *benefit* from a forced unity.

Without the alliance of democratic societies and Communists, the Axis war machine would prove invincible. In addition, had Germany not remained pinned down on the steppes of Russia, the D-Day invasion would have been "a gambler's throw."[4] We could not have liberated Europe without Stalin in the war. And Stalin couldn't beat Germany without Normandy.

Pragmatism prevailed even prior to Pearl Harbor. By 1940, the United States and Britain were funneling supplies to the Russians. Western food and equipment allowed them to stand when Hitler attacked with more than 3 million troops along an 1,800-mile front.[5] The Russian war sealed the doom of the Nazis by keeping them fighting on two fronts. *Unity, prevailing over differences, allowed victory.*

Takeaways from History

So what does all this war talk have to do with church multiplication? If we, the Church, could learn the lessons of 1943, we would have a fair chance of winning the battles we face today in fulfilling Jesus' Great Commission.

We are at war over the destiny of humanity. It is a spiritual war, just as the Scriptures tell us (see 2 Cor. 10:3-4; Eph. 6:10-13). For some, the concept of spiritual warfare represents a pre-scientific explanation of the human condition. For others, spiritual warfare is restricted to a highly personal contest pitting individual Christians against dark forces of evil— "I scratched my fender because the devil is out to get me."

These ideas end in *isolation*. The first stems from a conflict that is only imagined. The second understands warfare but isolates individuals in an attempt to live a merely peaceful life. But this battle is real, and it won't submit to our pet theories.

Spiritual warfare centers on evangelism—two forces wrestling over the hearts of humanity. It is both cosmic (the kingdom of heaven versus the demons of hell) and personal (individuals needing freedom from dark spiritual forces of bondage). It is a war that must be *fought strategically.*

There is much that we can learn from the Allies' victory in World War II. Three changes of thought, gleaned from the strategies and tactics of the victors of World War II, could benefit the Church's position in the battle to shine the light of the gospel into the world's darkness.

We Need a New Paradigm

As in 1942, we live in a world of doom and gloom. Church attendance has fallen off to just 26 percent, a long fall from the comforting 40 percent that we've all come to take as gospel.[6] Morality on television and in music is at an all-time low. War and the threat of terror stalk our dreams. The centuries-old war between Christianity and Islam rages stronger than ever.

Yet, like America in 1942, a kind of optimistic isolationism rules our thinking. We take comfort in the size of our very large and visible churches while ignoring the slippage in overall church attendance. Many even await the emergence of the next "Billy Graham" to keep the gospel visible in the West. Meanwhile, we don't plant churches fast enough to keep up with population growth, let alone think about saturating the culture.

We need to overcome the peaceful isolation of our comfortable church campuses. A missional church invades and permeates. The operative term is "Go," not, "Come." I can summarize isolation with a single question: "When was the last time you spent time hanging out with pre-Christian friends—on their turf and with their friends?"

We Need to Unify Our Forces

Isolation isn't the only thorn in our side. Like the Allies' strategy, we must surmount an idealism that divides the Body of Christ. We should rethink the unity of the brethren. We must be pragmatic about the need to unify our forces for a common goal. So ask yourself, *What is my attitude toward the emerging church? Toward my Roman Catholic brothers and sisters? Toward Pentecostals?* Or, if you are Charismatic, *What is my attitude toward the more Conservative wing of the Church family?*

Not heretics...

We must admit that we need each other. I can't tell you how frustrated I get when reading some of today's bright young authors. I question their logic and sometimes disagree with their theology; and their taste in clothing often reminds me of things that hung in my grandfather's closet. BUT, I thank God for them. I don't have to agree with them to *need* them.

Every spiritual climax the Church has ever experienced—from the events recorded in Acts 2, to the Great Awakenings of the eighteenth and nineteenth centuries, to the advent of today's fresh young thinkers—have upset established leaders, like many of my peers. When I was young, I vowed that I would not become a Pharisee in later life. Well, now I am in later life, and I willfully choose to engage and respect a rising generation of leaders. I will not put a bushel over someone else's candle after having begun my own journey demanding change.

And while we are talking about change, I confess that I've been attending Mass on an occasional basis. I've become friends with two Catholic priests in our neighborhood. We actually like each other. We publicly pray for each other's churches. And, contrary to much that I was taught as a child, I've discovered that they, too, believe they are justified by faith in the risen Christ.

I can't find any good reason to reject my brothers and sisters in Christ. I even struggle, because I realize I am *supposed* to love the guys who host all those websites attacking other Christians over minor differences in doctrine.

We must learn to love each other if we intend to influence the world toward Christ's love. If we can get over spiritual isolationism and divisive idealism, we can get on to the task at hand—*saturation evangelism*.

We Need to Increase Our Productivity

Here is where the lessons of productivity come into play. These are the primary lessons of 1943. There are two of them. First, we need an approach to evangelism that centers on church multiplication instead of addition. This is pretty simple: Stop counting converts and begin counting congregations. Second, we need a faster approach for producing the materials of spiritual war. This calls for relearning some old lessons about disciplemaking. These two changes could result in a strategy of spiritual warfare by tsunami. Much like democracies from 1943-1945, we could overwhelm the opposition with our numbers. It's been done before, and only ignorance or selfishness can keep it from happening again.

Human population multiplies relentlessly. As new technologies emerge, whole industries multiply. Meanwhile, Christians continue to think in terms of addition. We count converts and rejoice in the size of our churches. Small churches take refuge in the shadow of visibly successful, larger churches. This is a form of social isolationism that is losing the battle. The number of Protestant megachurches (attendance above 2,000) has mushroomed from 16 in 1960 to 1,210 by 1995. Those numbers doubled in just five years.[7] This sounds like great news until you consider the population of the country.

It has quadrupled since 1900, while the number of churches has grown by a mere 50 percent.[8] In other words, the population grew eight times as fast as churches could multiply. We are losing the war by not keeping up with production.

There is one exception. According to the Southern Baptist North American Mission Board, "Hawaii, where 13.8 percent of the state's population (1.3 million) regularly attends church, was the only state where church attendance grew faster than its population growth from 2000 to 2004."[9] Church attendance in Hawaii grew mostly because of rapid church multiplication launched by three individual congregations two decades earlier. Compare the stasis in overall church growth to the rapid proliferation of megachurches and you can see that we need another angle on our problem.

But lack of overall church growth and evangelism could change if we can renew our minds. At first, our efforts will be small and seem insignificant. But like anything else that multiplies, time and momentum are on our side.

However, if we want to see massive multiplication of congregations and Christians, we will need to sacrifice one of our most sacred cows—a professionally trained clergy. We are talking multiplication of congregations, not of seminaries. We haven't time to build enough schools to sustain serious multiplication (think of your church multiplying itself 100 times in a lifetime). To do the job, we'll need to revert to Jesus' method for multiplying Himself in a group of handpicked leaders. (More about that in a later chapter.)

Most pastors, me included, are concerned with making a good showing on the weekend. Why? So we can add members to our churches. This puts focus on two things, a great program and good teaching. I've had staff meetings where members of our team were totally bummed because of a bad transition from one element of the service to another. This happened in spite of large numbers finding Christ that day. I've heard pastors criticized for preaching too long, though a third of the church wept their way through the message. When adding members is our goal, we lose all biblical sense of priority.

Change the focus from addition to multiplication and strategy changes with it. Transitions are important, but less than before. The effect of the sermon grows more important than its length. In fact, the entire weekend is only a vehicle leading toward those relationships we call discipleship. It is disciplemaking that is *the key to everything*, "Any church that focuses on disciplemaking is by definition going to be a more authentic church."[10]

But this extends far beyond authenticity. My goal is to clone myself in as many people as possible. Not in some sadistic, authoritative way—but in the sense of "Follow me as I follow Christ." In this scenario, every mistake becomes a learning experience. Every tear is precious. Nurturing a movement outshines building a large church. I want to multiply converts, leaders, home groups and churches as fast as possible. Multiplication always trumps addition. I want to overcome Satan in my little corner of the world with radical disciples of Jesus Christ.

Some Very Good News

While the Western church is growing richer, it is gradually edging itself to the margins of society. That's the bad news.

The good news is that the non-Western church is multiplying quite rapidly. In 1960, 30 percent of evangelical churches were in non-Western nations; by 1997, that figure had grown to 70 percent.[11] The real growth of Evangelical Christianity in recent years has been in Latin America, Africa and Asia. Importantly, this is the result of intensive effort in church multiplication. *Newsweek* magazine estimates the birth of 1,200 new churches each month on the African continent alone.[12] In 1960, non-Western Evangelicals were about half as numerous as those in the West; by 2010 they will be seven times as numerous.[13] By 2050, only about 20 percent of the world's Christians will be non-Hispanic whites. Philip Jenkins, in his excellent book *The Next Christendom,* suggests, "Soon, the phrase 'a White Christian' may sound like a curious oxymoron, as mildly surprising as 'a Swedish Buddhist.' Such people can exist, but a slight eccentricity is implied."[14]

Even the concept of *foreign* missions is changing. By the 1950s, two-thirds of the 43,000 Protestant missionaries in the world hailed from the United States.[15] Today, 35 percent of all foreign missionaries are sent from North America, and another 11 percent hail from Europe. But those numbers are changing further. By 2050, more than 70 percent of missionaries will be from non-Western nations.[16] In fact, two of the three largest churches in Europe today were planted by Nigerians, and one huge Nigerian church can claim more than 6,000 church plants outside its home country.[17] South Korea now has 12,000 Protestant missionaries serving in other countries, more than any country other than the United States.[18]

Better yet, the 2006 goal of the Chinese underground Church was to place 100,000 missionaries into Muslim lands along the old Silk Road between Mongolia and Jerusalem. Mostly bi-vocational and underground, this "army of worms" still compares as a tsunami when held up to the estimated 40,000 to 50,000 American missionaries working overseas today.[19] And the largely rural Chinese Church is migrating to the cities as jobs become available. Because they so naturally form churches, this becomes another form of urban missionary activity. These people will plant churches.

Overall church growth is rapid. This is especially crucial in China as it emerges as the dominant player in the geopolitical world. It is estimated that between 20 percent and 30 percent of China's population will be evangelical Christians by 2030.[20]

Unfortunately, the less and less Christian West still controls the wealth and power of the world. And that's what this book is all about. With a little imagination, we can learn the lesson of the Allies' actions during the year 1943 and overwhelm an entrenched spiritual enemy by ramping up our numbers. To do so will require "manufacturing" thousands of new churches.

Some have described the necessary paradigm shift as a change from *seating* people to *sending* them.[21] It's a tough call and a daunting task. But it can be done.

2

KINGDOMS IN CONFLICT

• •

A SPIRITUAL BATTLE WE DARE NOT LOSE

Our post-Christian society still clings to basic Christian values evidenced in our democratic beliefs in the importance of the individual. But as the Church becomes smaller compared to the populace, those values may end up in the backseat. As keepers of the nation's values, the church finds itself providing national security. The nation is only as secure as its most basic values. Even as our current numbers decline, we still provide that security.

A Struggle Between Two Kingdoms

Evangelism and church planting are at the front edge of a conflict between two kingdoms. Luke describes Jesus sending 72 disciples to bless, heal and announce that His *kingdom* is near. On hearing of their victories, even over demons, Jesus remarked that He "saw Satan falling like lightning from heaven" (Luke 10:18). When the Church advances, the forces of darkness recede. Today, darkness seems to prevail over traditional Western culture. But it recedes wherever the Church is expanding.

This is a spiritual battle, not some kooky rant about demons in the closet, but a tug-of-war between two kingdoms. On one front it is fought by radical Muslims. On a second front, we find Chinese pragmatism funding wars in resource-rich nations around the world, "The tragedy in Darfur—and perhaps the future tragedy in Chad—is fueled by China's reliance on brutal regimes for access to oil."[1] The Chinese are the industrial imperialists of the twenty-first century. Another front is the never-ending battle against crime, drugs and pornography. Finally, postmodern humanists scream for the elimination of "intolerant, racist and bigoted" religion in the name of secular reason.[2]

The list goes on, but we had better believe that bringing people to Christ does more than add to God's kingdom. It promises to preserve our way of life—perhaps our very lives. It is good to remember that whenever the forces of darkness have prevailed in Western history, Jews and Christ-followers have come out losers.

Staying Focused on Disciplemaking

We can't afford to settle for any goal short of world evangelization. We must disciple nations. When Jesus said to make disciples of the nations, He wasn't suggesting that the Church make a few disciples in a few countries near Israel. Nor did He mean a few disciples in each nation. The command suggests transformation of the entire world.

Idealistic? Sure it is! But if you lose the ideal, you shoot too low. Politically correct? Probably not. But it is not imperialistic to seek to disciple the nations if you do it one heart at a time. This is not about grasping political power. Instead, it is all about the values of God's kingdom at the root of the society.

In the midst of huge cultural upheaval, Nigeria has quietly become the most Christian nation on earth. In that country, Muslims kill their Christian neighbors while Christians love their Muslim neighbors—the Christians are gaining ground. Love conquers all. The hope of the gospel is becoming the hope of the people.

At the beginning of the twentieth century the world was roughly one-third Christian. After shrinking late in the century, the church is growing worldwide. By 2050 some 34 percent will be Christians. And then as now, there will be about three Christians for every two Muslims on the planet.[3] "In 1900, the beginning of what American Protestants christened as 'the Christian Century,' 80 percent of Christians were either Europeans or North Americans. Today, 60 percent are citizens of the 'Two-Thirds World'—Africa, Asia and Latin America."[4] Though Pentecostals are growing the fastest in these areas, there are more than seven times as many Episcopalians in Nigeria as there are in the United States.[5] The president of the country is reportedly a believer. And they have done it without firing a shot. The country has its monstrous share of problems. But after you contrast the Christianization of Nigeria to the Islamic "revolution" in Darfur, we can discuss political correctness.

Of course we mustn't couch our mission in terms that make us look chauvinistic. This is why the temptation to link our gospel to a political party is so dangerous. A majority of evangelicals supported George W. Bush in both his presidential contests (though the vast majority of black evangelicals did not) only to have to wear his reputation over the war in Iraq. We cannot risk bowing to political pragmatism. We must stay on target to win entire cultures to the kingdom of God. This is a war in which love is the best weapon. It is also a war in which more soldiers on the ground equate to victory.

Activating ordinary people in very simple churches is how the gospel undercut the pagan Roman Empire in just three centuries. In the middle of the second century, a Christian leader would write to a Roman acquaintance, "We are in your towns and in your cities; we are in your country; we are in your army and navy; we are in your palaces; we are in the senate; we are more numerous than anyone."[6] A century later, these Christians controlled the emperor's throne. They did so while living under the terrible pall of bloody persecution. Love conquered in Jesus' name. They also did it by massively multiplying the number of disciples and mostly secret churches.

Examples of Christianity Leading Culture

Mention the intersection of faith and culture and someone immediately brings up the Crusades. Let's face it—the Crusades happened, and they were wrong. Some will debate that the Crusaders were not even motivated by an attempt to wrest Jerusalem from the infidel, but rather a Frankish attempt at real estate development.[7] And any sincere heathen will admit that the Crusades didn't reflect the teachings of Jesus. Nevertheless, the Crusades are a real and significant part of church history. The problem with Christianity is that Christians so often do it badly. The Crusades, the Inquisition and slavery sully our reputation to this day. But that unholy triad does not reflect the teachings of Jesus or the mandate to disciple nations.

When nations come to Christ, they build hospitals and schools, care for the poor and improve public sanitation. Morals improve, as does the quality of life, and a stronger economy usually emerges. Civil rights become important and "freedom" becomes more than an idealistic concept. It is interesting to note that roughly 27 million people live in slavery today, more than at any time in history—and that Christianity has become a (still very soft) siren against the evil practice.[8] Musician and political activist Bono said it well when asked why people need God:

> I look around at the twentieth century: It's not a great advertisement for unbelief. Where did Communism bring Russia? Look at what more openness is bringing to China. I will say this for the Judeo-Christian tradition: We have at least written into the DNA the idea that God created every man equal, and that love is at the heart of the universe. I mean, it's slow. The Greeks may have come up with democracy, but they had no intention of everyone having it. We have to conclude that the most access to quality in the world has come out of these ancient religious ideas.[9]

We are first called to disciple nations. While this most primary call is a spiritual issue, it also carries seeds of rescue from poverty, racism and evil dictators. Those are crucial needs. But these needs find their place parallel with the discipleship process. They seldom precede it. Remember, it was the background prayer and organization of Christians that burst into the so-called "Velvet Revolution" that brought down communism in Eastern Europe.[10] Following religious leaders into quiet prayer and protest, thousands eventually took their cause to the streets. When repressive governments failed to silence them, the tide turned in their favor.[11] Calm, underground disciple-making resulted in an earthquake that toppled the Berlin Wall. This bit of history represents the power of making disciples. To be sure, the external pressures exerted by Ronald Reagan and Pope John Paul II never hurt. But then again, these men were working from Christian convictions.[12]

Following the lead of John Wesley (1703-1791), and the tireless efforts of William Wilberforce (1759-1833), Christ's disciples overcame slavery in England and the United States in the nineteenth century.[13] It is interesting to note that one of Wilberforce's prayer partners was the "father of modern missions," William Carey. It was Carey who ushered in the reforms to repudiate the atrocious practice of "sati," or widow burning in India. Believing that the power of religion is inherently separate from that of the state, he progressed against this monstrous evil by bringing Jesus into the hearts of the largely unchristian rulers of India, both British and Hindu.[14]

A pastor named Martin Luther King, Jr., led the Civil Rights movement in twentieth-century America. A Polish Catholic named Lech Walesa led a revolution in his country. Today's Western journalists fail to note the strong thread running between religion, culture and politics, and that politics are ultimately a matter of faith.[15] The point is that positive world changes have usually followed large-scale disciplemaking.

Keeping First Things First

Salvation is not necessarily freedom from torture, or social improvement. It begins with a life-changing experience with God. It includes becoming a devoted follower of Jesus Christ. It is nurtured by membership in a local fellowship of believers.

For these reasons, a purely social gospel falls short. But so does a salvation that only includes a "decision" recorded on a card at an evangelistic crusade, or at the end of a church meeting. Paul went about the process of discipling nations in three simple steps: (1) he made converts (often coupling his preaching with the miraculous—what founding leader of the Vineyard movement, John Wimber, would have called a "power encounter"; (2) he made disciples of his converts; and (3) he quickly organized those converts into churches, appointing elders whenever he left the city.

Have you read the book of Acts lately? Do I need to point out that Paul spent mere days in some locations before being driven out of town? However, he usually left in his wake small, less-than-perfect congregations with ill-equipped leaders (by our standards). He kept up the coaching through letters—and he didn't have email. He had to communicate through an archaic messaging system that took months or years for round-trip correspondence. Yet that is *the* model set before us in Scripture.

We are in a titanic battle for the soul of the planet, and one that we dare not lose. When the other side prevails, disaster follows. We can't afford balance or neutrality—abroad or at home. The job *must* be done. We produce or perish.

Our recent history hasn't shown astounding results. We need to discover a new approach to cultural change. We need to find new angles of attack. The new ways are actually the old—the methods of St. Paul. Stick with me, and together we will unearth a simple plan for overwhelming our enemy with numbers. This is about *saturation church planting*. It is doable, and it's easier than you think.

3

THE BIG QUESTION

• •

WILL ANOTHER CHURCH REALLY HELP?

The New Testament depicts the Church as a living organism. Several of the metaphors for the Church include the possibility of reproduction. Reproductive abilities represent a sign of maturity in living organisms. They also represent the only way to preserve the species over time. Multiplication of the Church not only engenders greater evangelistic results but also ensures the survival of Christianity in our culture.

While no one would ever argue against the idea that the Great Commission involves multiplying believers, many become confused over the possibility of multiplying congregations. "Why not just grow the churches we have? There are empty church buildings all over the world. Can't we fill them before you start talking about planting new churches? I can barely lead my own congregation; what right do I have thinking about starting others?" Each of these statements implies a kind of self-limiting paradigm on the part of the speaker. To me, the answers seem as obvious as they are simple. The point is that the speaker would never take the risk of multiplying their church without a reason stronger than an argument from pragmatism. So, before we get to practicalities, let's look at the implications of some biblical metaphors of the Church.

Of Seeds, Vines and Vineyards

None of this will make much sense unless you are willing to acknowledge that the kingdom of heaven, the kingdom of God and the Church are loose approximations of each other in Jesus' mind. If you can buy into the previous sentence, then hang on for this ride. If your theology is too deep for that (for some it is), you might as well return this book for a refund.

At least seven New Testament metaphors of the Church (or Kingdom) suggest reproductive growth, with the first three being seeds, a vine and a vineyard.

Jesus described the Kingdom as a tiny mustard seed, which would grow to fill all the earth, providing room for the birds of the air to find shelter (see Matt. 13:31). For the seed to grow so large, it would have to multiply its trunk into many branches. Just prior to His passion, Jesus depicted Himself as a vine with all of us being its branches (see John 15). He then commands us to bear fruit, promising reward for those who do and punishment for those who do not. Any fruit includes the ability to reproduce the plant it came from. We sell ourselves short if we view this as simply adding converts to our existing churches. Reproduction is a key implication here. Then Jesus describes His kingdom as a vineyard where the workers are held accountable for the health and welfare of its many vines (see Matt. 20). He clearly expects to receive fruit from the vineyard and its *many* plants.

Paul uses family illustrations to describe the Church. He likens it to the Body of Christ in Romans 12 and 1 Corinthians 12. He portrays the Church as the Bride of Christ in Ephesians 5:22-33. And He describes *ecclesia* as the household of

God in 1 Timothy 3:15, as does Jesus in Matthew 18:17. Anyone living at any time in history would see the implication of reproduction in those three metaphors.

The final illustration is powerful because Jesus, Paul and Peter used it. This is the picture of a flock of sheep. Jesus lamented that the flock would be scattered when He, the good shepherd, was struck down (see Matt. 26:31). Paul encouraged the Ephesian elders to care for the flock of God, or their *local* and *individual* congregations (see Acts 20:28-29). He suggested that a shepherd should reap financial support from his flock (see 1 Cor. 9:7). Peter urged elders to feed their flocks and not lord it over them, but serve as good examples (see 1 Pet. 5:2-3). Sheep beget sheep, and wise shepherds manage sheep well enough that they need to create new flocks as reflected in the plurality of flocks that Jacob managed in service to Laban (see Gen. 30:25-43). When things got tough between them, Jacob moved his *flocks* a safe distance from Laban's *flocks*. Please note the use of the plural in the text.

So what's my point? Simply that the idea of multiplying our congregations lays just beneath the surface of much of the discussion of the church in Scripture. For us to miss this point leaves us forever trying to accomplish the Great Commission by *adding* souls to existing congregations. It leaves us hard-pressed to touch unreached peoples. Don't even think missions here. More than 25 million people in the United States have never heard the gospel. I submit to you that the New Testament *norm* is for you and me to multiply our congregations.

Healthy Mothers and Rapid Growth

Some creatures die during the reproductive process. Just pity the mate of the black widow spider, or imagine that poor salmon fiercely struggling back to the headwaters of her birth only to spawn and die. The good news is that most species and many plants become healthy, or at least stretch their reproductive years, through the process. And this is certainly true of humans as well.

Grandma Is Still Having Babies

Soon after purchasing our first house, my wife and I dug into gardening. Being young pastors, our financial situation was a little shy of anything you would call strong. With little money, we very quickly learned that we could fill our garden with cuttings from existing plants. What surprised us was the response of the mother plants. They often put forward two branches where we had snipped out the first. The first plant grew healthier through the pruning process. Jesus alluded to this in John 15 where He said we would be cleansed by pruning.

I've long since learned that multiplying our church prunes our congregation in some very healthy ways. Good people who are tired of their pastor and his message have a healthy opportunity for change (yes, there are people who've become *bored* with my great preaching over the years). Underutilized potential almost always goes out the door to morph into realized leadership for the Kingdom in the newly planted church. In fact, we've discovered some very strong leaders and even future church planters through this process. But we really hit the jackpot when we go about replacing those people with others.

Every time we plant a church, we make room in our own unique logistical equation for new people to fill the slots previously occupied by others. As these newly elevated leaders get their wheels under them, they grow and infuse us with new ideas so that we grow healthier through the process. Our congregation is over two decades old. We've birthed dozens of churches that have birthed hundreds more. We are much like a very healthy grandmother still capable of bringing new babies into the world into middle age.

Success in Those Early Years

On another front, consider the possibilities for filling the earth with the gospel. A decade ago, our congregation turned a 10-acre mountainside in Oahu into a terraced church campus with an ocean view better than most hotels on our island. In the process, we chose a groundcover only just introduced to Hawaii. A four-inch pot was selling for nearly $5 at the time. Our best estimate was that we needed 200,000 of these plants at a cost approximating a million dollars. Being church multipliers, we dug into our toolkit and came up with a plan. I killed off a 20-foot-by-20-foot section of lawn beside my swimming pool and planted 13 of those expensive plants. In the process, I multiplied them by taking cuttings from the mother plants. A few weeks later, we took more cuttings from newly pruned and rapidly growing groundcover. (Can you tell where this is going?)

Our college kids took over the task, eventually harvesting nearly a quarter of a million individual plants from that patch of backyard. Those plants, in turn, filled in well enough to cover our entire church campus. But notice also that the plants now in the ground are the end of the line. We don't harvest from them, so they will never be pruned. Most have grown "leggy" over time. They would be far healthier if they received the pruning of their forebears. Also note that these same plants were most healthy in their youth, before becoming overgrown. Churches operate in like fashion. They are most fruitful while young. Evangelism is a necessity to survival. It is only after congregations mature that they slow down, becoming less useful to the Master of the Vineyard. A helpful observation would be for you to ask yourself, "How many of the megachurches you know of are still pastored by the founding pastor?" The answer is, "Most!" Churches, like plants and children, usually grow the fastest in their earliest days.⌉

Picture with me a city like yours. How many "bare spots" are there where people do not serve the Lord? Can you envision your church taking cuttings from among your members and leadership systems to fill in those bare spots with new churches? Can you see how much easier it would be to adequately cover your city through multiplication than by trying to add enough members to your congregation to evangelize and transform your community? Do you see how ridiculous it would be for us 10 years later to be waiting around for those 13 pots of groundcover to spread themselves over our 10 acres? Apply that thought to churches. The only way to evangelize our community and our world is by multiplying our congregations. *Not the only way, but a great way.*

Underevangelized Populations

Let's consider some unique groups of people in the world. How would you get to people living in the scientific community at the South Pole? Or what about the tiny population of people who have all but dropped out of society to form a tight-knit surf culture along the southern coast of Japan? Did you ever see a baptism in the Persian Gulf? How would you evangelize Muslims in Pakistan? Or, how would you take the gospel to nomadic people who follow the grass with their herds in Mongolia?

We talk long and often of "unreached people groups" without realizing the full implication of that phrase. It doesn't always involve people on the upper Amazon or living along the Niger River.

In every case mentioned in the previous paragraph, our church has stumbled into a unique and spontaneous opportunity to spread the gospel simply because we've created a culture of multiplication. When one of our members got stationed in Antarctica, he planted a small church using me as the preacher through audio media. A young surfer girl moved to Japan, led some friends to the Lord and hooked them up with a new church we were already planting in the area. Our guys planted churches among fellow soldiers in both the Gulf War and the war in Iraq. I treasure photos of ocean baptisms in the Persian Gulf and of guys getting baptized in 50-gallon oil drums. Pakistan is turning into a church-planting paradise due to a chance encounter between a businessman from our church and a young Pakistani Christian. In Mongolia, our friends have churches that meet in those portable tents called *gheres*—though you may know them as *yurts*.

What about the bikers in your town, or the kids who've built a subculture around computer games? How about the people in a newly arrived immigrant group who are busy building a new life for themselves where you live? A church plant may be the best, or the only, way to touch those people. We'll talk about how to do it later and look at some modifications to your view of church that might make it easier. But for now, try to think of unevangelized or underevangelized groups on your horizon. Ask the Lord to give you vision for reaching them with the good news that God loves them and can give them a better life and a meaningful eternity.

The End of a Good Thing

It's a negative thought that all good things must come to an end. But it is true. Our planet will be reborn when the New Jerusalem comes to earth (see Rev. 21:1-4). This means that your favorite garden spot and your memories of a lovely sunset will be lost in the burning. A little closer to home, you and I will either pass from this scene and find ourselves planted in a very small farm, or we will go to meet the Lord in the air. Nothing is permanent. It's true of your church too. Congregations grow old and die, some more slowly than others. But all eventually die.

The only way to ensure the future of your church is to reproduce it, just like having children and grandchildren is the only way to preserve your own DNA. I travel a lot speaking about this with pastors. And I'm getting old enough that I have the perspective of history. I've watched countless congregations come to full strength in 10 or 15 years only to assume that the good times would last forever.

You know the churches I am talking about—those where the singles group are all in their 40s and the rock band members are in their early 50s. These people live like tomorrow will never come. They hang on to all that they enjoy as if it will last forever. They break my heart. Truth is, they do experience the wonderful grace and blessing of God. Trouble is, they will take it with them to the rest home.

One pastor friend of mine is still in the pulpit at age 78. Another just retired at age 75. Both are handing off a church of elderly people to a middle-aged pastor, hoping he will revive it into a youth movement like the one that birthed it so many years ago. It would have been better if they had each handed off to a much younger man a couple of decades ago. It would have been better yet if they had multiplied their own leadership among homegrown disciples and then multiplied their church by planting these carefully crafted leaders in new soil. The spiritual DNA of leader and church *are* valuable. In fact, they are irreplaceable. It is a shame to see them fall to death when they could live in the hearts and lives of many spiritual offspring. I am talking about both leaders and churches.

The Five Stages of Church Life

Long ago, someone wrote a song about a person who flourishes in the Lord, "They are like trees planted along the riverbank, bearing fruit each season without fail. Their leaves never wither, and in all they do, they prosper" (Ps. 1:3). This is true while we live. But it does not deny the basic facts of life and death, either in the lives of individuals or of congregations.

There are five, sometimes overlapping, stages in the life of any congregation, just as there are in your life and mine. These five stages are conception and birth, childhood and adolescence, the reproductive and childrearing years, middle age with its relative wealth and freedom and, finally, that slow decline of health resulting in death.

Conception and Birth

Someone, at some time, conceived your church. It probably took the form of a word from the Lord. For some it came as a painful result of a church split that could be likened to sexual assault. And some churches are born of rebellion that shares a commonality with teen pregnancy. But someone, at some time, conceived *your* church. It existed in their mind and heart before there was ever a public meeting. Then came the big day when a few folks or a lot, depending upon their prowess at outreach, got together, and the baby was born—either a small child or a large one. A church was born.

Childhood and Adolescence

Just like a newborn baby, your church at one time reveled in life itself. Most decisions had no precedence in the life of the congregation. They were precedent setters. There were no traditions. Then came adolescence with all its challenges. But by now there were some established patterns and traditions. Your church may have been unsure of its role in the larger world, but it also felt its own unique strengths and freedoms. It probably became very adept at certain types of ministry and built an identity around its talents much like a young woman builds an identity around her good looks, or a young man around the kind of car he drives.

The problem with churches is that many of them stall in this stage of the life cycle. No, they cannot avoid middle age and old age, but they never progress into adulthood along the way.

Churches that stall in adolescence probably outnumber those that go ahead and give birth to another church. They are like the young men that America once categorized with the term "Peter Pan Syndrome." These are people who refuse to grow up. Just check the surf scene in California to witness this. Or go visit Japan where the latest trend among women is to reject the idea of marriage, choosing instead to remain in their parents' home while holding down a good job and outfitting themselves in Gucci. Peter Pan churches latch on to some strength and then magnify it to the point of near distortion. They build identity around their great music team, their wonderful choir or their powerful ministry to men. These are all good things, but all destined to age and pass if they miss their opportunity to invest their special talent and ability in a new (and usually younger) congregation.

Reproduction and Childrearing

The best case for reproduction is that it preserves the race. We are told that people fall in love for chemical reasons, ultimately submitting to a subconscious biological urge to package their genes along with those of another into the great gene pool of humanity. Bunk! Human reproduction is the result of emotion—of passion. Sometimes it is illicit, but mostly it is born of intense love between two people. It is a love so intense that it fairly demands sharing it with another—hence the birth of a child to live in the blessing of that love.

This is much the same as the birth of churches. They are born of passion. Some are surely born of illicit passions, like anger or rebellion, but most are born out of love between people and the Lord—a mutual human love emanating from God in their hearts. When Christians awaken to their ability to share this love with the world, it becomes most natural to give birth to other churches. Some need a little coaching along the way, but the reproductive act is the natural outgrowth of the love in a healthy congregation.

So is the nurture of the offspring a reflection of love between the parents and love between them and Jesus Christ. One of the most positive experiences you will ever know is to announce to a parent congregation the newest growth steps of a recently planted church.

Middle Age and Empty Nesting

I have been pastoring since the early 1970s. The first congregation I planted is definitely approaching middle age. The one I pastor now is just 12 years behind. In both cases, we are much like a grandmother still having babies. We enjoy the success and relative wealth of middle age while we have yet to stop multiplying our congregations. We enjoy watching the churches we have birthed multiplying while we continue in the process ourselves. In one situation, we go nine generations deep with church plants. Often we now only *hear* of the birth of great-great-grandchildren after the fact. No one consults us about the conception. It is a great feeling.

Age became a benefit when we learned that we could challenge our "daughter churches" to think about giving birth by the very fact of our continued example. I assume that we may one day stop having babies and eventually fall into decline, but I also assume that our continued birthing keeps us healthy and will stretch our fruit-bearing years for a very long time. Our current situation calls for me to plan to step aside from the senior pastor role into a role of pastor of seniors. In other words, I will keep pastoring the people I've always shared life with while a new generation takes the helm. Our biggest task is ensuring that the next generation in our own congregation is committed to continually multiplying our congregation around the planet.

Decline and Death

I watched my grandparents age, and then pass away. Their generation took this process much more in stride than did my parents. And I am sure that my own peer group of baby boomers will go out kicking, screaming and digging our fingernails into the pavement around us to yet a greater degree. My parents are attentive to their family and to their health in ways that my grandparents were not. I have watched them battle together against my mother's heart disease and now bravely against my father's Parkinson's disease. They are tough, loving people, and I want to learn everything I can from them in this phase of life as I did in every other.

With rare exception, every congregation will age and die. Some will see their buildings outlast them as an historic monument or even as an art shop or a bar. But the life they have known eventually ends. The questions I always ask at this stage are, *Did they live life for all it was worth while they had the chance? Did they leave a legacy through the birth of at least one other church?*

What goes for individual congregations holds true for movements. My denomination is booming around the world. We now number more than 50,000 churches. The original congregation that kicked it all off, Angelus Temple, has found new life. It is once again a spiritual force in Los Angeles. But we are nearly stalled across the United States. We close about 90 churches a year in the United States, and we open just a few more than that. Some have the vision to multiply, but many do not.

Change the Paradigm

Some churches with the vision don't know what to do with it. Any way you look at it, we need to change our paradigm or settle for slow decline and death as a movement. The choices are pretty clear and very stark. Although we've slowed, we haven't yet gone into reverse. There is still hope if we grab the handles of opportunity that are available.

The practicalities of church multiplication far *outweigh* any fear we have about having never come this way before, violating the current tradition of our movement or losing a few dollars for a few weeks in the offering while we adjust to the absence of some of our prime members. There is a great big world out there awaiting our actions to grow our churches exponentially. The only way I can see to do so is by multiplying my church and my leadership.

What do you see?

HOPE

. . . .

IMPERFECT PEOPLE MOVING IN THE RIGHT DIRECTION

Yeah, the world's a mess. But it doesn't need to remain that way. You picked up this book because you believe that your church has the right stuff. You believe that your church deals the goods that our ever-more-spiritual-and-frightened-by-terror world needs.

The good news is that you are not alone. You share faith with growing millions of others on this small planet. However, there is a severe shortage of people who would bother to pick up a book with a title like this one. We could use an army of new congregations, churches like yours—imperfect but moving in the right direction. Churches that understand that "love never fails" (1 Cor. 13:8, *NKJV*).

The great news is that your church *can* multiply! You can multiply your efforts by multiplying your congregation again and again. And, since we are not cloning, you can multiply new churches without building in the problems you probably face in your current situation. The harvest fields are ripe. The time is now. Continue reading, implement the suggestions, and come join a movement that is changing the future history of our civilization!

Church Trends in Some of the Most Unlikely Countries

Church multiplication touches every country in the world, including Islamic nations. New churches now mushroom in places like China, South Korea and Nigeria. Even Nepal, in spite of its political troubles, is showing some of the most rapid church growth in the world.

I've spent time in Myanmar with severely repressed pastors bent on multiplying churches until they overwhelm their culture with love from the inside out. The problem is that Christianity is shrinking in the wealthy West. Meanwhile, America, the great funding agent of Christian mission, is well on its way to following Europe into an enlightened paganism. Unless we wake up, missions as we know it will begin to fade worldwide come mid-century.

The earth suffers from a severe shortage of potential church multipliers like you. Yet, hope sails on the evening breeze. Even Europe now sports several small but rapidly growing church multiplication movements. Nicky Gumbel's Alpha studies are making a difference not only in England but also throughout the continent. Groups like Christian Associates International launch congregations in public schools, community centers and borrowed church buildings at odd hours. A growing number meet in houses or apartments. Australia's Hillsong Church is planting in Europe. The Awakening Chapels, basically a house church movement, has hurdled the Atlantic with strong success. A few newer congregations even gather in pubs.

These people multiply churches because they believe the gospel is the only hope for a Europe torn by racial unrest, threatened by terrorism and lacking an anchor for its collective soul. The new churches in Europe are but a down payment on a necessary spiritual awakening.

There Is Still Some Salt in American Soil

In the late 1940s, Europeans adopted a post-Christian world-view while cleaning up the battlefields and bombed-out cities of two world wars. Traditional Protestant countries drifted from Christianity in the economic cesspool that followed the war. Today, even hard-core Catholics are turning away from church. Church attendance has dropped by half in Ireland over the past 25 years, while Spain is busy loosening the bonds between the government and the Catholic church.[1] European attitudes toward the gospel have hopped the Atlantic, rooting themselves firmly in our soil over the past few decades.

The United States still pumps out more missionaries, and prints more Bibles, than any other nation. It boasts bigger churches than it ever has, while overall church attendance in America stalled two decades ago.

A study conducted by researchers at the University of Maryland, in the late 1990s, shows only about 26 percent of Americans attending church on a regular basis.[2] A more recent study by the North American Mission Board of the Southern Baptist church is more chilling. It reports that a little less than 20 percent of Americans are actual churchgoers, and by 2050, church attendees will have fallen to about one half of the 26 percent involved in 1990.[3] And the Bible is becoming a forgotten book. Even as the American church stretches toward the brass ring of political power, rising generations in our country cannot clearly tell you who Jesus Christ is—or the meaning of His death. And they most certainly do not believe in His resurrection or the freedom it brings.

Yet, overall spiritual interest is stirring. Jesus still makes the cover of the major news magazines every Christmas and Easter, as do issues like the running conflict over creation, homosexuality and abortion rights. The presence of a growing number of Jesus parodies on *MTV* and *Comedy Central* at least show that Christianity is still an issue in our culture.

The United States is currently the fifth largest mission field in the world.[4] The tide of the old Christendom is running out—and maybe running out for the best. We need a new perspective, and one that allows us to operate from a minority position, much like that of the Church during the first two centuries.

The good news is that in America, as in Europe, there are still thousands of Christians (like you) who believe that we can reverse the tide of recent history. They see church multiplication as the key. The church is God's operational base for transforming culture. It comforts the brokenhearted; it also emboldens the courageous, those who will weave the social tapestry of our cities and neighborhoods. Churches assimilate and conserve converts. More churches equates to more Christians, which means more salt in the earth.

We need more churches like yours. But we also need churches unlike any we've seen for a while. We need churches that are comfortable with a *minority* role in society. We need members who are unafraid of persecution or mockery and who are operating in the power of the Holy Spirit. In other words, we need to look more like the church in the first century.

Think Like the Early Church

While the term "postmodern" first appeared in the nineteenth century, postmodernism took root in the United States shortly after the Second World War. Americans today are postmodern thinkers, rejecting moral absolutes, scientific reasoning and the Scriptures as philosophic pillars for living. They are also functionally post-Christian. They came up in a world that has increasingly marginalized our churches and our message. Though many Americans still describe themselves as Christian, the percentages are lower each year, and the United States is now the fifth largest mission field in the world—the largest in the Americas.[5] Some would say that we live in a neo-pagan society.

A New Worldview

This translates into a new reality for us. The logic that converted recent generations is out the window. You don't need to—and you actually cannot—scientifically prove the existence of God. The arguments and apologetics of recent decades don't appeal to people who simply do not accept the possibility of absolute truth—or even "true truth." For many, every point of view has its own value and none rises above the rest. The one caveat here is that younger people tend to believe strongly in a spiritual universe. They are impressed when that universe intersects their own lives. Mercy-oriented prayer can be a frontline evangelistic tool, softening even the hardest heart.

We cannot expect rising generations to "return to church" as did the Baby Boomers, beginning with the revival of the 1970s and continuing through the attraction of large seeker churches at the turn of the millennium. That influx reflected a generational reaction against dead church traditions. Boomers rejected dusty traditions but retained the worldview of their childhood. Today, many of our largest churches lament the lack of members under 30 years of age. The Boomers had church experience and a basic knowledge of Scripture. Returning to church was possible because they had been there in the first place.

Current rising generations know little about Jesus Christ. They also see Christians through the eyes of the secular media. We wear the stereotype of judgmental and negative people who impinge on their personal freedom. Gandhi's statement pitting Christians against Jesus has become popular, "I like your Christ, but I do not like your Christians. Your Christians are so unlike your Christ."[6] Some of this reaction is undoubtedly rooted in reality; some is imaginary. Either way, the solution is a new generation of churches led by people who found Christ in a postmodern, post-Christian environment. The West needs a host of fresh young leaders who instinctively communicate with their own generation.

But Not So New, After All

Today's spiritual climate is nothing new to the Holy Spirit. We are beginning to approximate the cultural conditions faced by Christians during the first three centuries of church history. Neither is this climate much different from what people face on a daily basis in East Asia. What *is* different is the fact that cultural Christianity ruled America for so long that today's mature Christian leaders have difficulty envisioning an environment where it has gone missing. Unfortunately, this causes us to hunker down and wait for the emerging generation to "wise up" and return to a gospel they never knew.

Who Will Carry Out the Vision?

The good news is that there are probably several culturally attuned, potential church planters in your church, as there are in most churches. These are mostly younger people. They may be critical of some of your most cherished ideas and traditions. But it is young people who bring drastic changes to society. Revolutions are the product of young hearts, minds and energy.

Two of the key generals in the American Revolution, Henry Knox and Nathaniel Green, were 25 and 33 years old at the outbreak of the war. George Washington, himself, was only 43 years old at the outset of the conflict.[7]

Twenty-five-year-old Knox, a colonel at the time, was crazy enough to attempt to haul 34 mortars and 24 cannon more than 300 frigid, snowy miles from Fort Ticonderoga to Boston. They were to be carried by huge sleds, except for the hundred miles that they traveled by boat over partially frozen lakes. The mortars weighed a ton each, while each cannon tipped the scales at more than 5,000 pounds. Most thought the plan unworkable and Knox a crazy young upstart. Fortunately, Washington did not. Knox succeeded, making possible Washington's victory against the British in Boston.[8]

Perhaps you are, or you know, a potential Henry Knox, just wild enough to attempt the impossible. Better yet, you may be a potential George Washington, possessing enough faith and clout to pave the way for the young radicals among us. We need more of both.

We will discuss new churches for a new generation in chapter 20. But for now, realize that it is visionary people—people like yourself—who are needed to pave the way for those who will go out to multiply your church both geographically and generationally.

All you really need to begin multiplying your church is vision. The Lord will supply whatever else it takes. But, of course, vision is sometimes tough to come by. Yet without it, we perish (see Prov. 29:18).

Vision is much easier when you can see through the eyes of someone who has already traveled the road. That is where this book comes in. Abraham was called into a land that God identified as his inheritance. But he went without knowing exactly where he was going. You may be called into an adventure without knowing exactly where you are going. You do, however, have a multitude of counselors in the books you find on the subject. Often their job is to simply clarify vision.

I recently spoke to an amazing convention of pastors in Brazil. They've planted a thousand churches in the state of Pará. Beginning in Belém, a city of 1,800,000, they now extend into the upper reaches of the Amazon to places only accessible by boat or air. They've planted 400 churches in Belém alone— and many of these congregations number in the thousands. The movement now owns an airplane, enabling ongoing coaching of barely literate pastors in jungle villages. My job was to convince these amazing people that the increasing wealth of their nation carries the possibility of them evangelizing other continents in the coming decades. They went for it.

I got a laugh when I explained that Brazilians could safely live in certain places where I, as a white-faced American, might enjoy a life expectancy of about seven seconds. Then they got serious—very serious. After the meeting, some said they would pray for secular job opportunities in other countries with the aim of reproducing the movement they enjoy in Brazil. Two men stood out to me: They said they would pray for opportunities in North Korea and Saudi Arabia.

Their example is one of vision quickly embraced. It should bear viable fruit in years to come, especially because these people so naturally make disciples and start churches relationally rather than institutionally.

Stop Adding and Start Multiplying

Multiplying churches is not hard. We just make it that way. Take a moment to sit back and ask, What could happen if I invested the rest of my life in the process of discipling nations by multiplying churches? Just to make it more fun, let's pretend that money will never be a problem. Our only problem is finding vision for the task at hand. Ask the Holy Spirit to give you vision. Write some notes. Turn them into a prayer log. If you ask, the heavens will surely open.

The world is multiplying while the Church adds (at best). But addition can never keep pace with multiplication. Multiplying starts slow and small, but with time builds momentum that addition will never touch. Don't be content with addition! If we are so satisfied with the "success" of addition, we will never venture out into the deeper waters of multiplication.

The power of multiplication is obvious: You see it in nuclear chain reaction, pandemics and even roaches in your basement. What would you do if one million people came to Christ in your area this year? The questions haunt me and dictate the way I spend my energies.

Multiply your current goals by 100. If you do not have ministry structure or systems to reach that new goal in a relatively short time, you are not set up for rapid multiplication. Just as you cannot slowly adopt the metric system, you cannot evolve into more reproducible systems. You must die to the old and put on the new.

Consider Paul's admonition to Timothy in 2 Timothy 2:2. He holds out for passing on the teaching to four generations of faithful leadership: Paul . . . Tim . . . faithful men . . . others also. His standard led to thousands of years of influence. Don't even think of calling it multiplication unless you can identify the fourth generation in a discipleship network! Any strong leader will attract other leaders. Because they are leaders, they will have followers, and you can easily reach three generations of influence without actually multiplying yourself. To get to the fourth generation (the people Paul called "others also"), you have to give yourself away to your disciples like Jesus did.

PART 2

INSIDE THE WALLS
OF OUR MINDS

5

LEVERAGE

· ·

MAKING THE GREAT
COMMISSION DOABLE

Jesus' Great Commission in Matthew 28:19-20 is a tall order. Many pastors live under a cloud of guilt because their efforts toward its fulfillment seem to consistently fall short. In fact, this is true of the entire Christian church. We are always looking at that goal as unmet.

Some have even given up on the Great Commission as a doable task, surrendering to the idea of merely building the largest congregation they can in hopes of making a *small* difference. This is perhaps most true among leaders of smaller churches. This form of stewardship still falls short and leaves us feeling short. Multiplying our churches is the only realistic way to approach the Great Commission. It's all about leverage. Our problem is as old as the gospel itself, we still lack enough labor to bring in the Harvest.

[handwritten margin note: with more # 's at least]

Answer this question: Would it be easier to grow a church stalled at 80 members, to 400, or would it be easier to launch five churches that might grow to 80 persons each in a decade? Multiplication opens new realms of possibility.

Leveraging Your Influence

A wise man once wrote, "Two people can accomplish more than twice as much as one; they get a better return for their labor" (Eccles. 4:9). I recently experienced an example of this truth as I was helping my neighbor and his wife repair their small floating boat dock. The contraption is basically a wood deck built on top of a half dozen large plastic barrels. One barrel had slipped out and broken free from the frame during a heavy storm. I'm new in the neighborhood, and trying to make friends, so I offered a hand at what seemed an impossible task. They were trying to force a large air-filled barrel under a heavy floating motorized raft. The raft relies on these barrels to stay afloat.

My neighbor had positioned his wife on the opposite end of the raft, hoping to lift his side of it out of the water enough to *slip* the barrel under the raised structure. But they lacked enough leverage to do the job. When I volunteered to help, he positioned me next to his wife on one end of the vessel, leveraging our combined weight. At first we nearly capsized the raft. Together we had leverage that neither of us could have had alone. Once we learned to balance the thing, we easily lifted the contraption enough that my friend could slip that obstinate barrel underneath with one hand. Our combined weight could accomplish far more than that of either of us operating singly.

There is a lesson in this for the church. What is impossible for a single congregation gets easy when more become involved. I'm not just talking about church unity here. What would happen if you were to double the number of congregations in your town? What if you could multiply your church 10 times, or 100? What difference could you make if you really set out to make disciples of all the nations? Leverage is the key to Great Commission success.

The writer of Ecclesiastes went on to say, "A person standing alone can be attacked and defeated, but two can stand back-

[handwritten margin note: As long as the non-negotiables are shared between the churches]

to-back and conquer. Three are even better, for a triple-braided cord is not easily broken" (Eccles. 4:12). Let's paraphrase it: "Two have a better chance at victory in spiritual warfare than one; and a bigger team is better than a smaller one."

Again, leverage comes to mind. I learned this lesson as soon as we planted our first daughter church. My disciple immediately became my peer. Something healthy happened in our relationship that strengthened both of us. And my own church took on a new sense of victory knowing that we had multiplied ourselves into two strong congregations.

The lesson came home in a greater way when we began planting churches in Honolulu. We set out to reach 1 percent of the population of Hawaii, in churches we had started or helped to start, in 10 years (Easter attendance). This took place when only 4 percent in the state identified themselves as Christians. It took us 11 years to reach the goal. As a bonus, our activities stimulated the launch of two other church multiplication *movements*. Along with the three movements, several individual congregations have launched one or two churches. Better yet, some of those leaders who currently plant churches were the very people who resisted the idea (and us) in the beginning.

When we started, we couldn't rent public schools for church services because of a legal snag. That got resolved, but today we face the same problem, but for a different reason. We now have difficulty renting a school to plant a church because there are churches meeting in virtually every school in the state. Some schools host three separate congregations on a weekend. As a result, we are now learning to launch house churches.

Have you ever noticed the shrinkage that takes place through mergers? In business that shrinkage is the intended purpose. You merge two entities, lay off redundant people and build a more profitable company. But mergers often break down, and they may never result in the joined entity taking a broader share of the market. In order to gain market share, a company needs to open lots of branches or get into franchising its operation. Joining two businesses can result in less than the sum of the parts, while hiving off new locations enlarges profitability. In other words, you *subtract* by adding two entities together, and you *multiply* by dividing them.

The same is true in church. If you merge two Bible studies, a month later you will net fewer people than you started with. Merge two congregations and the same thing happens. But if you multiply a Bible study by dividing it into two, what do you have in a month? More people! The same holds for churches.

If you've adequately trained leadership, you are on your way to the Great Commission by making disciples and sending them out to multiply your church. Evangelism is not as difficult as we've made it.

I like to think of this process as "equip and release." Not too different from fishermen who "catch and release." Most churches think of equipping people so they can serve the organization. They want to keep them. It's more fun and far more productive to train leaders and then release them to multiply the Kingdom.

Why Should You Care?

I have a suspicion that you are a lot like me. You often lay awake at nights worrying about how to leverage the influence of the gospel in our culture. You probably try to assess your own limits. The conversation in my head goes like this: *Just how much of the world am I responsible for? I know I can't touch everyone. But how much is enough? What will earn me those words, "Well done, good and faithful servant"?*

Well, I can't argue your limits before God. I'm not even all that sure of my own. I do know this. I am not responsible for the whole world. But I also know that I am responsible to do all that I have with the hand the Lord has dealt me. I can pastor only so many people. If I knew how to pastor more (in my own church) I would. But I don't. Meanwhile, multiplying our church has allowed me to leverage my somewhat limited gifts to touch a whole lot more people around the world than I would have by beating my brains out trying to grow our church.

Exponential Growth Is Possible

Church multiplication carries the potential for exponential growth of the gospel. We see this all over the world. Churches that multiply cover greater geography with their message. Those that don't remain confined to a given locality.

I recently spoke with a pastor in Myanmar who struggled to see the multiplication factor as viable in his hometown while operating it in the countryside. His congregation had launched more than 100 successful churches in a rural state but not a single one in Yangon, the capital city (formerly known as Rangoon, Burma).

When I asked why they didn't multiply congregations in their own metropolis, he didn't seem to understand the question. He answered, "We are a big church, and we *are* reaching the city." When I compared the size of his very large congregation to the 6 million people living in that city, his eyes lit up. He suddenly saw the potential for exponential growth in the influential center of his nation. I think he will feel a lot more fulfilled after he begins multiplying churches in Yangon, as well as in the countryside.

One of the most exciting things about multiplying our own church has been what it does at home when we hear news of victory in our church plants. *Enthusiasm* and *momentum* are priceless commodities. They are the common returns of church multiplication. I sleep better knowing that my congregation is excited about the gospel.

The excitement quotient rises with every testimony of grace in one of our church plants. It is especially high during those months just before and just after we send out a crew to start a new church. We usually grow in number enough that we fill up within weeks of launching a new church. I believe a stalled congregation can nearly always grow its way back to momentum by preparing for and launching a new church. The process is invigorating.

In fact, I've watched some pretty unhealthy churches get well through church multiplication. The story goes like this. A church is dying. Some discontented people get an idea to start a new church in order to escape the squabbling and entrenched positions. Meanwhile, someone grows wise enough to dub the separation a birth rather than a split. The proud parent (church) gleans fresh life from the birthing process.

One of my church multiplying friends maintains that some churches should never think of multiplying lest they "clone their unhealthiness." I maintain that such a condition can change through intentional multiplication. Few have ever cloned a church. Most church planters choose the best characteristics from even an unhealthy congregation to use as building blocks. There are very few churches that are too unhealthy to reproduce.

To take this a step further, we should think back to the Protestant Reformation. Luther, in his idealism, broke from the prevailing state church because of what he saw as extreme ill health. Yet he used its basic structure in igniting the birth of a host of new congregations.

Exhaling Is as Important as Inhaling

Your body wouldn't survive if you never learned to exhale. Fresh oxygen turns to carbon dioxide in the blood. It becomes a poison that can kill us. Interestingly, plants breathe carbon dioxide, giving off oxygen as they "exhale."

What is true of your body is also true of the Body of Christ. Your church needs to exhale every so often in order to remain healthy. Space won't permit me to tell you all the stories of the "pew-sitters" who have gotten involved every time we have launched a church.

Whenever we multiply, we send out a significant number of active and fruitful leaders. Some of those who leave have grown stale in their slot in our church. But the move invigorates them—it also clears the way for someone with fresh vision to take their place. It has become a hobby of mine to watch for formerly underactive members to arise and take their place. Exhaling members allows for the fresh wind of the Spirit in our midst.

The Community Benefits

As I've mentioned, our church has been around for more than two decades. While we've planted churches, we've also grown into one of the largest Protestant congregations in our small town. And our job is getting easier. We now enjoy the partnership of the newer congregations in our locale—those we started and those we didn't. As we band together, we strengthen each other's resolve and are able to bless the community in ways that none of us could do alone.

cool

Fellowship between pastors has a long tradition in our town. But the newer churches are the ones stoking the flames of evangelism in the rest of us. I am thrilled knowing that there is a growing cadre of labor ready and available for the harvest in our community.

As I write, one of our "granddaughter" churches, in another community, just announced that they are launching a new church in our town. We already have two churches of our denomination in a town of just 40,000, but together we reach fewer than 10 percent of the people. We can't wait to welcome the newcomer.

So, What Should You Do?

If this book lights your fire, you should begin praying that your church will multiply. Pray for God to show you a like-minded person to share your growing vision. Better yet, form a discipleship circle around this book—read a chapter a week and discuss it, praying over the conclusions you draw. I promise you, God will show up and something good will come of it.

6

CONFUSION

· ·

WHY DON'T OUR
CHURCHES MULTIPLY?

Most churches think of multiplying by planting another church as just another option—a rare option. They may even believe that God is asking them to do so but they feel unsure and are waiting until they are stronger before attempting to launch the first new church. Let's face it: multiplying a church can be a scary task.

We often fear losing members to a new church because we are naturally protective of the congregation God has entrusted to us. On another front, we can be loaded down with worry at the very thought of being responsible for the success of someone we have discipled. We may feel unsure of how our peers will view us if we start launching churches. I've talked to pastors who were criticized for "trying to start a new denomination" just because they launched several churches over a course of a few years. We may even be so bent on building a megachurch that we've forgotten that God still gives back to those who give (see Luke 6:38).

However, if we think this way, we will overlook the fact that churches that multiply usually grow because they are constantly pruning the bush, making room for newly emerging leadership.

Why Church Multiplication Is the Exception

I've always wondered why church multiplication is the exception rather than the rule. Over the years, I've spoken at conventions and seminars for many different denominations. I always want to go as a teacher sharing principles that I've learned. Sadly, I usually find myself actually cast as a motivational speaker, brought in to help "get things going." You've probably noticed that more pages in this book are devoted to motivation than to the how-to angle of church multiplication. This is because while most leaders of spiritual movements are hungry for church multiplication, pastors don't seem to share their inspiration—especially those pastors with surplus resources.

Some think the problem comes from selfishness. These people judge pastors as trying to build their own little kingdom. I mostly don't buy that reasoning. Sure, I've met some very selfish leaders—kings protecting their little fiefdoms. But they are the exception, not the rule. I think the primary reason we don't multiply churches is because overworked pastors see church multiplication as just another program. Overly busy pastors already feel overwhelmed. They just duck whenever anyone approaches them with another project.

This problem may actually lay in the "program orientation" that has become one of the chief drivers of the modern church. We see the church through the eyes of the last seminar we've attended or the latest denominational mandated system. We look to books and seminars on leadership for new methods for ministry. We should instead search the Word of God for long-term strategy and culture-crossing tactics. Deep inside, we know that a programmed approach to world evangelism won't cut it. But we are products of our culture. A media-driven business model thrives in Western church thought. Unfortunately, church multiplication is *not* part of that program.

To get out of the rut, we need a longer look at our Christian past mixed with a hard look at our own demographics. Whenever the church has prevailed in history, it has been on the heels of a church-planting movement. Evangelism without new churches equals frustration and a culture filled with believers slip-sliding away from their conviction. Add new churches to the mix and you get a force for positive change. This force operates from within the culture.

On the demographic front, the idea of any wholesale change to the surrounding culture induced by simply adding new members to existing churches is highly suspect. To disciple nations requires full-blown spiritual awakening. Any real move of God will include Paul's tools: evangelism, discipleship and the rapid multiplication of churches and leaders. The church in the West is pretty good at evangelism and discipleship. We score very low in rapid multiplication of churches and leaders.

Tools vs. Rules

Whenever the church looks to its own biblical roots, it changes for the better and for the long-term. When it aims at the latest program, it reduces itself to decisions that endure only as long as current social trends. I think the reason we don't plant more churches is that most of what we do is curriculum oriented while discipleship is based on relationship. Just ask yourself if you really think it is possible to design a 'one-size-fits-all' curriculum for church planters. I don't.

I recently spent several hours with a man who had resigned from a high-paying job as an instructor for folks wanting to learn how to multiply churches. He said that his particular movement had just *mandated* that every church planter in their denomination had to go through the curriculum he had designed. He quit because his very helpful curriculum had just become a rule instead of a tool.

We all know that the law kills while the Spirit gives life (see 2 Cor. 3:6). This man quit his job because his material had become "law" to those he had hoped to help. His hard work and vision had been denigrated to "just another program." Braver than some, he moved on. He now operates a highly relational network of disciple-makers who've launched many successful churches. Do they use the tool he built? Yes, but only if and when it's appropriate.

Multiple Opportunities Demand Multiple Solutions

Don't forget!

Church multiplication must be led by the Spirit. One group may plant in a tough urban neighborhood, another in an affluent suburb. Yet another may plant in a rich country such as Japan, even while their friends decide to involve themselves supporting church multipliers in an emerging nation such as Mongolia. Tougher yet, how about those who plant churches in Islamic nations? For another twist, you should meet my friend who has planted two congregations among street gangs on our Hawaiian island.

The point is that you can't use the same approach in sophisticated European cities that you would in a place like rural Cambodia. I've witnessed successes in all these areas when local leaders focused on discipleship within their own culture; the ability to minister just seems to flow from one person to the other. The wisdom learned tends to be universal and work just about anywhere. Meanwhile, the methods differ widely from culture to culture.

When you trade away relational discipleship for a programmed approach, the job grows quite complicated. It becomes impractical, perhaps impossible. Curriculum design is always a challenge, and teachers can bog down in form rather than function. If you are to really grasp church multiplication, you must rethink the whole idea of disciplemaking at a local church level. It will have to become your most important task (I think Jesus implied that it already is).

Growth vs. Growth

What we are looking for when we think of church growth? Are we looking to build a big church? Are we hoping to convert the entire world? Are we content with transfer growth from other churches? Would we be happiest living in a rapidly growing new subdivision where most growth comes from people moving from other congregations because they moved into our neighborhood? Is our idea of foreign missions summarized in monthly cash offerings for people in faraway places? Or does our congregation actually multiply itself overseas? Answers to these questions reflect our own views toward a world that is truly lost without Jesus.

Churches grow biologically and families have babies. This is addition. Another form of addition occurs when members transfer from other churches. But even conversion growth is actually addition. When newly converted people join our congregation, we are still adding names to our role. While addition is good, it doesn't compare to multiplication. And we've learned that it won't disciple nations.

On the downside, there is a zero-sum game that looks like addition but isn't. This is where a leader uses personal notoriety to create a network of churches by adding existing churches to their circle. I saw a website that invited churches to fill out a form online to join their relatively new denomination. Don't get me wrong. I see value in churches banding together. But building a network does not necessarily grow

God's kingdom. It is like moving money between brokers and pretending that you are investing. Not much changes.

It's About Conversion Growth

I think we should be thankful for any kind of growth we can get. I certainly want the Lord to add members to our church in any way He chooses. And conversion growth is especially important.

Every time we read summary statements in the book of Acts, they include conversion growth. In Acts 2, we read about 3,000 people being added to the church. By the time we reach Acts 4, either 5,000 men were added to the church or the total number of men had reached that sum, without measuring the women and children. Acts 5:14 tells of multitudes being added to the church due to the miracles that followed on the heels of the deaths of Ananias and Sapphira.

Shortly after the church scattered, due to the stoning of Stephen, we read about the citizens of Samaria becoming believers "with one accord" (Acts 8:6, *NASB*). When Peter ministered at a place called Lydda, he healed a man sick of the palsy, causing all who dwelt at Lydda and Sharon to turn to the Lord (see Acts 9:33-35). Shortly after that, Peter brought the dead woman Dorcas back to life and "it was known throughout all Joppa; and many believed in the Lord" (Acts 9:42). When Peter found out that the Gentiles could be saved, he preached to those of the house of Cornelius and "Even as Peter was saying these things, the Holy Spirit fell upon all who had heard the message" (Acts 10:44).

I could go on. But I think you get the point—it is conversion growth that we are after. But even conversion growth is simple addition, and it never substantially changed the culture of ancient Israel, let alone the Roman Empire.

Even More, It's About Multiplication

Real multiplication only happened after Saul of Tarsus hounded the Christians out of Jerusalem. We read, "All the believers except the apostles fled into Judea and Samaria" (Acts 8:1). They ran while the "courageous" apostles continued to disobey the command to go into all the world and preach the gospel.

The believers ran, but not quietly: "The believers who had fled Jerusalem went everywhere preaching the Good News about Jesus" (Acts 8:4). And they traveled far beyond Samaria and Judea:

> Meanwhile, the believers who had fled from Jerusalem during the persecution after Stephen's death traveled as far as Phoenicia, Cyprus, and Antioch of Syria. They preached the Good News, but only to Jews. However, some of the believers who went to Antioch from Cyprus and Cyrene began preaching to Gentiles about the Lord Jesus. The power of the Lord was upon them, and large numbers of these Gentiles believed and turned to the Lord (Acts 11:19-21).

This is one of the most significant passages in the New Testament. It is here that the Jerusalem church, *without* the evident blessing of the apostles, multiplied itself. The unnamed believers from Cyprus and Cyrene planted new congregations in new soil. The result was a church that would go on to aggressively multiply congregations throughout the Mediterranean world.

It was at this point of forced multiplication that Rome began to tilt toward the gospel. The movement was so small as to remain imperceptible. Nevertheless, the ground moved under the feet of those scattered followers of Christ.

These people were the crucial link in the chain of truth through the centuries. Without them, Rome might never have become Christianized. You might not be reading this book. In the end, it was the sheer force of numbers that overwhelmed the Roman Empire, and it happened because the church multiplied itself. Just like the Allies in World War II, the good guys simply out-produced the spiritual forces around them. They waged spiritual battle by tsunami. And they won.

Why don't we multiply churches? Because we don't understand the importance. But even those who understand the importance of Church multiplication still face significant roadblocks to the process, as we'll see in the next chapter.

ROADBLOCKS

· ·

WHAT STANDS IN OUR WAY?

Okay, so you get it. You want to multiply the church, but you haven't started. What stands in the way?

I recently put that question to a friend of mine. He told me that his pastor had a vision for saturation church planting in one of the capital cities in the United States. Their goal was to evangelize the entire city through church planting. So far so good!

We had both spoken at the same seminar and he bit into the vision I shared. But my friend, supportive as he was of his pastor, knew the plan wouldn't accomplish the task. It would not work because the goal of 100 churches was a great start but still too small to evangelize that needy city. My friend had researched the demographics; his pastor had not. The problem was that the vision was too small. They would need closer to 400 churches to accomplish their goal.

Four hundred church plants is a tall order in anyone's lifetime. But it's not impossible. It costs no more to challenge people to start 400 churches than it does to challenge them for 100. Vision like this has a built-in multiplier. Once a movement engages large goals it will attract the attention of others, bringing allies to the task.

Big goals inspire large teams. So where are the roadblocks? They are *in our mind.*

My friend's story is again helpful here. Together we outlined several tools for expanding his church's vision to reach their city. Then he dropped the bomb: "None of this will work. Our elders will never go for it. It violates their views about church."

To this point, dear reader, you may be asking, "What are those views?" But first, maybe we should ask, "Who are *those* elders?"

The elders in that church are institutional thinkers who fear loss of control. They are good and godly people. But they have a stake in the status quo. In this case, it was a sentimental stake—they saw things as they always were. And they were most comfortable with familiarity. A radical rethink about the nature of church is nowhere on their radar. Even the goal of 100 churches would push the limits. This was not about politics; they simply couldn't let go of *emotional* control.

In some other cases, the obstacles can be a little more sinister. We all know leaders who don't want to lose political and financial control—they feather their beds by controlling others. Their tools are licensing and ordination issues, bylaws and the like. Whether driven by emotions or politics, institutional leaders have attitudes about what is proper in church life. These attitudes remain major roadblocks to saturation church planting that could change a culture.

I'm still on the esoteric side of the discussion, but stick with my reasoning. Follow me back to Normandy on June 6, 1944. The Germans had three basic lines of defense: underwater barricades, the beach with its minefields and the armed soldiers themselves. The underwater barricades, with explosives attached, would destroy unfortunate landing craft. The beach was a fortified maze, bristling with everything from minefields and barbed wire to massive antitank barricades. And then there were those thousands of well-equipped soldiers with their artillery pieces pre-sighted to the landing beaches. These three lines of defense were more than 400 miles long—a coastline fortress that the Germans believed impregnable.

Conventional logic lay with the Germans. But unconventional logic prevailed among the Allies. Had Allied leaders believed Hitler's Atlantic Wall fail-safe, they would never have attempted the invasion that liberated Europe. The *institutional* leaders of the time were desperate. They were also innovative. Their innovations destroyed the enemy fortress in a single day.

Buildings, Bucks and Brains

Like those Allied war planners, our institutional church leaders must turn innovative if they plan to disciple nations, beginning with our own. We must find the weak spot and exploit it in every way possible. I believe that weak spot shows up every day in humanity's quite credible search for meaning, purpose and community. Television ads sell cars by attaching personal significance to the product. Extreme sports highlight the satisfaction we derive from singleness of purpose. Online communities are mushrooming to fill people's need for touch.

How we meaningfully address those very human needs constitutes our perception of a "proper" church (and how to launch one). Our perception of church is one of our greatest strengths. However, it could also prove to be our greatest weakness.

The enemy's primary defense perimeter against the rapid multiplication of churches may well lay between our ears. Let me take you back to my friend and his church with the goal of planting 100 churches. After he told me that his elders would never go for our unorthodox ideas about church multiplication, I asked him a question: "So what root issue stands between your church and saturation church planting in your city?" His answer was threefold: "Adequate buildings, money for salaries and a field of adequately trained pastors."

Buildings, bucks and brains are often in short supply. Inadequate resources in those three areas are Satan's security against saturation church planting. Isn't it interesting how a spirit of poverty targets resource, relationship and revelation—all of which are liberally promised in the Scriptures? The enemy has us feeling inadequate right where we ought to find our greatest adequacies. The outcome of our fears is huge!

The three fundamental roadblocks to church multiplication constitute the logistical issues we must overcome. But let me stress, they are the *least formidable* obstacles. The attitudes we hold about them are more significant. Our own attitudes are the weak spot in our offense. And they are the soft spot in the enemy's defense. They halt us before we ever attempt to sort out the three more visible roadblocks of buildings, bucks and brains. But, here is the good news. You can eliminate roadblocks by changing attitudes. If you can promise your institutional gatekeepers that you can eliminate the buildings, bucks and brains issues, they may very well push their attitudes aside and partner with you to launch a church-planting movement.

There is a growing frustration within Christian circles with the pace of evangelism. Younger followers of Christ also hunger for "something more" in terms of experiential faith. In the West, we are gradually realizing that we might have lost something that our developing-world cousins still possess. If you visit churches in Africa, Latin America and even Asia, you will encounter a gospel that still includes the miraculous. The dried-up rationalism of Western Enlightenment thinking seems nowhere to be found.

This growing angst seems to tilt toward church multiplication. A raft of new authors now call for a return to New Testament principles and practices. We are slowly concluding that the Early Church had something going that we should emulate instead of improve. We are beginning to realize that the book of Acts presents a prototype, rather than primitive, church.

Returning to the New Testament example instead of to denominational practice for instructions immediately whittles away those three weighty costs to the rapid multiplication of churches: buildings, bucks and brains. In light of Paul's church multiplication ventures, church-owned real estate, full-time salaries for pastors and seminary educations seem less important than they used to. This is crucial, as all contribute heavily to the financial overhead of Christianity.

Buildings

For the past two or three decades, churches that are multiplying themselves have looked to rental property for meeting space. Importantly, many of these properties have been public buildings that only require a few hours each week of rent money. With that, another piece of overhead bit the dust. The current outburst of churches starting in homes effectively reduces this cost to zero for churches choosing this avenue of reproduction.

Also, churches started in homes can help us cross cultural boundaries. Postmodern Western Christianity is largely a middle-class phenomenon. We've found that the ultra wealthy live in a world unto themselves. In my experience, many of these people would more easily attend an informal fellowship in a home or high-rise than attend church with a bunch of people who share their values and opportunities. As to reaching poorer communities, again the home is an asset. I have a friend in Austin, Texas, who trains middle-class white professionals to launch home churches in the Hispanic barrios. They must radically adapt to their chosen mission field. But when they do so, they bring their contact networks into play, helping people with legal and financial problems along with bringing the gospel to them.

In the past, the building issue was fought on the battlefield of pride. Leaders resisted the "storefront church." Today, we hold church in everything from warehouses to shopping centers. I am pressing you to take it a step further. Launch churches wherever you have people, *not* wherever you can rent a building. Start in a park, if necessary; that's how we launched the church I currently pastor. I have a friend who launched a highly successful church in Shinjuku Park in Tokyo. They kicked off under handheld umbrellas during a typhoon. Eighteen months later, they were able to rent a building—a bar. It snowed on their final Sunday in the park. They began by meeting under umbrellas and they ended under umbrellas. Yet, during those 18 months they grew to more than six times the size of the average congregation in Japan. People like innovation. When we overcome the need for a conventional building, we open ourselves to all sorts of unanticipated benefits.

Bucks

The cost of a full-time pastor is a huge barrier. In the past, our congregation spent a lot of church-planting funds on pastor's salaries. The overall cost to us was catastrophic whenever a church plant failed. We felt that we had squandered God's money. Finding a way to eliminate this cost would allow us to plant more churches with the resources at hand.

It's necessary to separate *operational* costs from *opportunity* costs. An operations budget includes overhead items like rent, salaries and equipment. An opportunity is a rarity that usually presents itself whenever you do something truly "new." Think in terms of this question: "Why not spend all the money you have drawing a crowd to the first week or so of a new congregation?" Fund the opportunity and let the results of that opportunity (the crowd you attract) fund ongoing operations. Whatever you do, don't squander start-up funds on overhead.

In an ideal world, a church launches with a bang. It evangelizes hundreds of people in the first few weeks and is on its way to mega-church status. And this often happens—but not often enough.

So what do we do when the new church is small and finances are tight? In America we are used to funding the pastor's family and other operating costs from the missions budgets of parent churches or denominations. One of the problems with this method was that it fostered a welfare mentality in the new church. A mindset of perpetual dependence often results in resentment toward the very people funding that dependence. Not a good thing. Another problem was that the pastor was chained to relative poverty, as was the sponsoring organization. Resources were strained at every level, and the idea of saturation church planting remained a myth.

The good news is that this reality is changing. Church multiplication networks everywhere now work with "bi-vocational" pastors. This means they receive a small remuneration from the church while maintaining a secular job. Costs are vastly reduced to both the sponsoring church and the church plant. The pastor usually earns more than if the church funded him or her alone. I even know a pastor of a relatively successful church who morphed the congregation into a network of house churches. They grew by 50 percent in a year, after nearly 10 years of history and 6 of stagnation. He restarted his construction business and now earns far more than he did while pastoring full time. Did I mention that this man is a seminary graduate with a better quality education than mine?

With money becoming less of a problem, a new church can afford to do creative things to serve its community. The results are evangelism and health.

There are other benefits. The membership enjoys having a pastor who is more in touch with the world they face in their own jobs. Beyond that, a bi-vocational pastor is in a great space to evangelize in the workplace. This creates an ongoing example for the congregation through personal illustrations from his own seed sowing. Finally, a bi-vocational pastor seldom needs to accept the excuse, "But, I'm too busy" from one of the church members. The pastor can counter by saying, "Look at me, I'm busy, too, but I find time to serve Jesus." Bi-vocational pastors bring financial capital to their situation. They also bring a certain leadership element that a paid pastor does not.

Brains

The New Testament promotes a hands-on approach to education. Discipleship is the natural tool for leadership development. At its best, it is both relational and experiential. We learn by watching others and doing what we have watched.

In this model, seminary becomes an adjunct *tool* for people who have already made their way into leadership. It is no longer the gateway into ministry (nor the restrictive hole in an hourglass). It remains a useful option, but definitely an option. Change it from a rule into a tool and it becomes a handy thing to have around instead of a costly roadblock to rapidly multiplying the church.

Conversely, seminary as a *rule* functions as a huge obstacle to the opportunities that exist. Face it: seminary is a great opportunity if you can afford it. But, you have to be *able* to afford it. The high cost of higher education keeps many otherwise capable leaders from even considering the thought of launching a new church.

The main costs are fourfold: money, time away from family, time away from ministry and time spent on something that turns out to be the wrong career choice. First there is money. Seminary, along with all other forms of education, has become the purview of the well-off or those willing to dance with an education loan for the rest of their life.

The second cost is time away from family and business. The best way to judge ministry potential in any person is to look at his or her family and business. The problem is that those with a healthy family and any success at business, while they would probably make an excellent pastor, are simply unable to devote the time necessary to complete seminary. Their family and business preclude it.

A third cost is time away from ministry. My experience has been that proven leaders who enter seminary always make ongoing ministry a lower priority during the time they are in school. Too often they drop out of ministry altogether because they are so busy with their studies.

Fourth, there is that hidden cost born by those who attend seminary faithfully, turn in all their assignments, score well on tests, graduate and then fail at pastoral ministry. I know people who view themselves as failures because they "wasted" three years in seminary and then did "nothing" with their degree. Never mind the fact that they are solid, faithful members of their churches. The expectation that three years of study equaled a spiritual gift takes a huge toll on people.

There is a fifth cost worthy of our attention. That is the loss of potential leadership among people who may possess keen spiritual gifts of leadership while lacking scholastic ability. For instance, the best person to evangelize in the backwoods of Kentucky might not have sufficient education to even enter seminary. Or what of recent immigrants or impoverished people living in our inner cities? Educational requirements can, and do, preclude valuable ministry and church multiplication across the land.

So what about seminary? Am I saying to junk it? No way! Seminary is a valuable tool. But, it is just that, a tool. It is our perceptions about it that hurt us.

Keep seminary for young people whose parents can afford to fund it. Or for mid-career folks who've burned out and are looking for a safe space to heal. At the same time, make room in your system for church planters who have been trained on the job in a local church. Finally, after a congregation launches, teach their leaders to fund continuing education for their pastor in terms of both time and money.

We've taken this approach in our church for years. Not all of our pastors go to seminary. However, all do *learn the ministry* on the job through disciplemaking in relationship with someone more mature and experienced. We've started a lot of churches that would never have existed if we had made seminary a prerequisite. I can find six models of education in the New Testament; only one of them mentions the word "school."[1]

Freedom Bound

The great news is that these three options—an alternative to church buildings, bi-vocational pastor leaders and suspending educational requirements—make it easier to start lots of churches. On the other hand, they can become a new form of limitation if we aren't careful.

We would not allow philosophic bondage to house churches any more than we would be bound to church buildings. I don't believe that every pastor should have secular employment. Nor would I eliminate formal education. We should always choose to be freedom oriented. This requires that we choose the "and" rather than the "or" when making decisions. Let's just get on with multiplying disciples and churches, using any and all available tools.

Having found freedom from rents and mortgages, many in the house church movement *intentionally* limit congregational size, tilting toward rapid multiplication. To some, it is anathema to meet in a church building or with a large congregation. It seems more reasonable to launch a church in a house than to allow the Holy Spirit to dictate its ultimate size. Is a pastor bi-vocational or paid a full-time salary? We do whatever works, depending on the unique combination of gifting, community size, employment opportunities and congregation size. To matriculate or not to matriculate, that is "a" question, but it is not "the" question. Seize the opportunity. If seminary presents itself as an option, it is a wonderful option. But training by discipleship is definitely the mainframe New Testament approach.

These choices are particulars. God's great universal is the command to get out into the world and disciple nations. Let's get past the roadblocks and on with the task. Either method has its merits. Remember that Bill Hybels, founder and senior pastor of Willow Creek Community Church near Chicago, started without a formal theological education, as did evangelist Greg Laurie, founder of Harvest Crusades and pastor of Harvest Christian Fellowship in Riverside, California. Both were trained on the job by their mentors. Senior pastor of Saddleback Church in Lake Forest, California, Rick Warren, graduated from seminary but launched a church in his living room. These are exceptional examples, but they underscore the blessing of flexibility.

Some Additional Roadblocks

The big three roadblocks we've already examined account for most of the reason that churches don't multiply. But there are other roadblocks that are less common but still significant. Let's look at three additional impediments to rapid multiplication of churches. These are pirated leadership, past failures and complicated structures that cannot be reproduced.

The Roadblock of Piracy

A good place to begin is back with my friend whose pastor wants to plant 100 churches. This wealthy church plans to hire 100 seminary graduates from across the country. They have employed a headhunting service to search for the best and brightest.

To me, this is a formula for failure. For one thing, it is a shot in the dark to import leadership, because of cultural land-mines within the church and the surrounding community. And this is one of those communities where culture is a very big deal. Do it their way or hitch a ride out of town. The second problem with imported leadership is piracy. Piracy may work for Disney films and Johnny Depp in the Caribbean, but it seldom blesses the kingdom of God.

Few people go to seminary without the sponsorship of some other pastor or significant leader in their life. I don't mean someone who signed a letter of recommendation, but someone who mentored them. In many of these situations, the prior relationship had hopes and dreams attached to it. There were plans for these seminary graduates to return home, eventually pastoring the churches of their youth. Or, the plan may have been to plant a church from the congregation that sent the person to seminary. To disrupt those plans is piracy, plain and simple.

What gives a single church in a single city the right to skim the cream of our seminaries for itself? Who says the rest of the country deserves nonfat milk when it comes to emerging leadership? Do you understand my use of the word "piracy"? I can think of no better term to describe the disruption caused by this kind of thinking.

Besides, the pirating church does itself a disservice. It will never know the legitimate pride of raising leadership organically. It won't know the joy of launching a church with a person who was born again, cleansed from iniquity and discipled into leadership—all of it locally. This congregation may succeed in evangelizing their city, but they will never spawn a self-reproducing movement. Whatever they build will die with the charismatic leader who drives the process.

The Roadblock of Past Failures

Failed attempts come back to haunt us with the words, "We tried that before and it didn't work . . ." But past failures are not etched in stone. Our church made three solid attempts at launching small groups before one finally "took." Later, I read in a couple of books that most churches need three attempts to get it right. I didn't know whether to be happier over our success or the fact that we weren't alone in the two previous failures.

Failure can be crippling. But it shouldn't be. Apply the "been there, failed at that" logic to your dating life and you would never have gotten married. Tell a couple who want to get pregnant that they should quit trying due to past failures. My point is that you and I should never surrender leadership to our past.

We can profit from mistakes by analyzing and learning from them. This is one of the weakest roadblocks to church multiplication. Yet it is the one I hear most.

If you've failed, you need some advice. The best advice I can find is implied in Scripture where it says, "Steady plodding brings prosperity, hasty speculation brings poverty" (Prov. 21:5, *TLB*). Don't give up. Get up and give it another go.

The Roadblock of Impossible Structures

Babies are small, and they are born without complete knowledge of the universe. The same can be said of healthy new churches.

We've added a lot of machinery to that simple relationship called "church" we received from the apostles. A friend told me a heartbreaking story that will overstate my point. He's a church multiplication coach for his denomination. One Sunday he visited a tiny new church that had insisted on spending most of their denomination-furnished start-up money on a sound system. The equipment was great. The band wasn't so hot, but they were working on it. What had him grinding his teeth was the fact that there were more people on the quite large worship team than there were people sitting in the audience. To him, they were all dressed up with no place to go.

But I'm not just talking about technology. We operate large churches much like Wal-Mart operates stores. We attempt to do *everything* for our clientele. This is fine when the size of the community and the dynamic of leadership permit it. I am not opposed to megachurches; we operate our own congregation as a "full-service" church. My problem with our model begins with the expectations we place on our church multiplication efforts. Too often, would-be pastors believe they must duplicate all our organizational and technical hardware from their first week of operation.

I've heard it put another way: "After all, a baby has 10 fingers and 10 toes just like its mother. It's only natural that we should offer everything you do." But is this really an appropriate metaphor for a new church? Or is this dangerous thinking? Sure, my kids had all their appendages in place when they came out of the womb. But they didn't have the skill sets or the tools they do now. No baby comes out of its water world understanding, say, calculus or investments. Likewise, no baby church ought to expect to operate a full-scale counseling ministry or the hottest children's church fresh out of the box. Any new congregation ought to offer teaching, fellowship, prayer (and its results), praise, generous giving and evangelism outside its four walls. These are the basics displayed just after Pentecost (see Acts 2:41-47). I believe they are the fingers and toes of the ministry. The rest of the stuff is optional. It has to do with skill sets that are acquired over time. To create expectations around them is a case for more failure than we want to endure.

This is no plea for low-quality service. It is a cry for limiting the services offered. You do the best you possibly can, but you focus the energies of the newly minted church toward the essentials. I know of a huge, full-service church that has launched one church plant in two-and-a-half decades. The daughter church is huge. It had a massive advertising budget to start (though I suspect much of that advertising drew members from other churches). Its musical offerings are some of the best on the planet. It evangelizes large numbers of people. But it is an "it," not a "they." Because the parent church held the bar so high, it can only afford to replicate itself once in a blue moon. Contrast this to the efforts of Paul in Acts 13–19, and you will see my point. Some are calling for a renewed simplicity in the way we do church—a return to God's process for making disciples.[2] I pray that we heed their call.

In a war, you need both artillery and foot soldiers with rifles. Our large churches represent heavy artillery. But artillery is nearly useless without infantry. Do you know what you call an artillery unit without infantry? It's a "defensive position." It stays in one place trying to repel a mobile enemy. Our megachurches carry some pretty heavy firepower. But add a few hundred infantry units in the form of new churches and we set ourselves up to attack the enemy's defenses.

I hope that every church we launch outgrows our own. But I won't wait to guarantee that before launching others. This is a numbers game, pure and simple. We need to outfight the enemy in his own strongholds. For that reason, we never attempt to clone our church. We only birth babies and then coach them into the best they can become according to their own unique gifting, skills and demographics.

Leave the Roadblocks Behind

Roadblocks are made to be moved, to be hurdled or to be run around. Hitler tried to hide behind his "Atlantic Wall." But we simply overran one position then poured massive numbers of men and arms through the opening. That was the turning of the tide for the war. On the eve of the event, General Eisenhower stood alone in the valley of decision. He faced a deeply entrenched enemy, weather that threatened to capsize his ships and a corps of general officers often at each other's throats. His response: "I am quite sure that the order must be given . . . okay, let's go."[3] In other words, he made a choice. It would have been a catastrophe if he had failed. It was a wondrous decision because he succeeded.

Roadblocks do exist. And they inevitably involve risk. But inaction only prompts losses. To paraphrase Eisenhower, "I am quite sure that a decision must be made . . ."

8

EMOTIONS

• •

IT DOESN'T FEEL
QUITE RIGHT

The final roadblock is so important that I want to give it its own chapter. This is that background feeling of unease that so often holds us back from faith. It's hard to call it unbelief; it's more like a "fiery dart of the wicked one" (see Eph. 6:16).

Do you ever feel like there is a cloud over your head while planning or executing ministry strategies? If so, welcome to the club. Misgivings abound in the kingdom of God. Many successful leaders are suspicious of their own success. Most feel undeserving and wonder how they got there. Anyone with any experience in this area can tell you that feel-good emotions are generally missing as they slog on to victory.

D-Day, the battle for Normandy and the retaking of Europe, tends to live on in a kind of glorious memory in the hearts of those who were spared by the heroics. These significant events look even better at the movies. However, the men who lived through them seldom spoke of them, except, perhaps, to one another. When they did speak, they were often embarrassed or even put off by medals and descriptions of the Greatest Generation. To them, these were hard-won battles and a long boring walk across a continent punctuated by moments of terror.

Church multiplication can seem similar to warfare. There are lots of days filled with the single motive of perseverance. They are punctuated by threats to the very existence of the new congregation and rewarded with outbursts of blessing and growth. The process never actually gets to "feeling right."

If you wait until it all feels right, you probably won't do much of anything, much less multiply yourself in a group of disciples or multiply your church. This is a matter of vision morphing into New Testament processes.

Frozen in Place

Did you know that armies often used bicycles during the Second World War? Weather permitting, a bike could help a messenger move quickly and was something of a difficult target to hit. Even the British and German infantries sometimes moved troops by bicycle. I recently had some thoughts about this when I saw a couple of bicycles frozen up to their axles in snow that had alternately melted and frozen again over a period of a few days. I was in Sapporo, Japan, enjoying the beauty of a fresh snowfall when I came upon the bikes. These bikes were frozen for the duration. You couldn't get them out without breaking, melting or destroying them in some other way.

The experience caused me to think about my own emotions. They run hot and cold—melted and frozen depending on the situation. My emotions, like snow, can be pretty or they can freeze me out of God's action plan for my life.

The bicycle owners had made a crucial mistake when the snows first appeared. Perhaps there had been a couple of days when the snow didn't stick. Or maybe they just got lazy. Either way, lethargy left their bikes useless while other bicyclists were regularly traversing the white stuff as they went about their daily business. The bikes didn't have to get stuck.

They got that way through inaction when action was the order of the day. The problem with those Sapporo bike owners is that they settled for ownership rather than ridership. In an unholy mix of metaphors, they got off the pony and left it to freeze to death.

I've lived through two seasons of renewal—the 1970s' "Jesus Movement" and the rapid proliferation of Christians and churches over the past three decades in Hawaii. From my perspective, each season only looked victorious or like renewal as we looked back on it. But it never *feels* quite right while we are going through the day-to-day activities of evangelism and church multiplication.

Sparrows Against the Bismarck

Often our greatest efforts feel puny compared to the obstacles we face. Without God's grace and power, we would surely lose the battle. But God does come through. Miracles do happen. Buildings do become available. City fathers do bring their blessing. The list goes on.

I often find refuge in the Lord's encouragement to Zerubbabel, who oversaw reconstruction of the temple: "It is not by force nor by strength, but by my Spirit, says the LORD Almighty. Nothing, not even a mighty mountain, will stand in Zerubbabel's way; it will flatten out before him! Then Zerubbabel will set the final stone of the Temple in place, and the people will shout: 'May God bless it! May God bless it!'" (Zech. 4:6-7). That's the way it is, we move *without* much human strength or political power, yet God gives increase and much is accomplished.

The word of the Lord to Zerubbabel continues: "Do not despise these small beginnings, for the LORD rejoices to see the work begin" (v. 10). Our beginnings are often small, and we feel insignificant. I recently ran across a bit of history that reminds me of heaven's abilities attaching themselves to our weakness. It is the story of the sinking of the most sophisticated and powerful battleship ever built.

The German battleship Bismarck was the greatest battleship ever built, but it lays barnacle-encrusted on the bottom of the North Atlantic. It's very sinking proved the ineffectiveness of large fighting ships against small airplanes launched from carriers. But this story is even more dramatic when you dig beneath the surface.

The Bismarck destroyed England's greatest warship in its first week at sea. In a single day it took down a cruiser and England's largest battleship, the Hood, which was the pride of the British fleet. The loss of morale in war-torn London was greater than the loss of the ship.

After three days of searching, the remains of the British Navy found the Bismarck, only to lose track of it in a storm. When sighted again, the Brits threw everything they had at the Bismarck, all to no avail. Finally, a squadron of World War I biplanes launched a desperate attack with air-dropped torpedoes.

You read that right, these were *World War I biplanes* up against the most sophisticated bit of war machinery in the world. The planes were little more than propeller-driven kites. They were also England's last naval hope. The Bismarck under attack had gathered a pack of submarines to its defense. Had the British attack failed, both the Bismarck and the U-boats would have put the remains of Britain's fleet on the sea floor.

But one tiny biplane hit its mark. Better than just a hit to the ship, it struck the rudders of the great beast. Bismarck could only swim in circles. Two days later, the most powerful battleship that would ever be built lay on the bottom of the Atlantic. The sinking and attendant battle drew German submarines away from a convoy of 22,000 men and material bound for the campaign in North Africa where Britain would win its first land battle of the war. The hand of God was at work, sparing the world the horrors of Nazi domination.

It couldn't have happened without the daring of a single pilot who flew "too close" to his prey, risking his life to murderous anti-aircraft fire to toss a small torpedo at a monster.

We're talking David and Goliath here. Not just in terms of size and armament, but impact. The work of that lone pilot enlivened a nation deeply in need of hope.

I wonder what that pilot was thinking as he lifted off the deck of that carrier. He must have been praying pretty hard. His tiny aircraft was no match for the giant he would attack. He had no armor to protect himself against the anti-aircraft fire soon coming his way. His offensive weapon was a single torpedo, many of which had already struck the ship only to explode harmlessly, leaving just a dent to record the death of a brave pilot. Had that pilot turned back or made a half-hearted pass at the ship, the war and world history would have turned out much differently than it did.

Much the same can be said for the brave souls who would seek to disciple the nations. Our presence is often flimsy at best. But we do not walk alone. We stand in the fear and strength of the Almighty. It makes all the difference in the universe. "If God is for us, who can ever be against us?" (Rom. 8:31).

PART 3

IN SEARCH OF
SCRIPTURE

9

MODEL

• •

JESUS AS A CHURCH PLANTER

If the word "apostle" means "one sent on a mission," then Jesus was the first apostle. He was sent on a threefold mission. First, He was to reveal the Father as "the word became human and lived here on earth among us ... the glory of the only Son of the Father" (John 1:14). The second leg of the mission was to invest in His disciples, leaving them the task to "go and make disciples of all the nations, baptizing them in the name of the Father and the Son and the Holy Spirit" (Matt. 28:19). The third phase of His mission was to organize those disciples into the unit that met in an upper room on the Day of Pentecost. That unit was a church; hence, Jesus was a church planter.

...seek & save That which was lost... Luke 19:10

Jesus planted the church at Jerusalem. His model and the task He gave those disciples eventually became the model for the apostle Paul, and it is our model today if we will accept it. Jesus came to teach us to multiply the church.

Some will struggle with my calling Jesus the first church planter because they hold that the church actually began on the Day of Pentecost. But from a practical standpoint, what would you call the groups of people in Galilee that believed Jesus' message prior to His death on the cross? Did they return to their synagogues unchanged? Or did they have a special relationship, formal or informal, with other believers in their community? What would you call those 120 congregants in that upper room on Pentecost morning? And what would you call the leader (I'm not talking Peter here) who drew them together in the first place? Whatever your theology, Jesus was the first viable church planter.

Learning from the Past

Waging war requires careful planning and is built upon a solid knowledge of history. From the tactics of thirteenth-century Genghis Kahn to the battle history of the latest wars, generals and colonels invest a lifetime of study hoping to build strategies that succeed. *Good idea*

The church is very aware of spiritual warfare. And we, like the military, seek strategies for success. The problem is that our strategies often fall short of the order of battle. We seek to live an overcoming life. Or, we seek to influence a few people around us. We may even pray for God to show us how to grow our church so large that the surrounding community takes notice and many come to Jesus. We strategize neighborhood literature blitzes and stadium-filling evangelistic crusades. All of this is wonderful, but it often replaces the goal of the kingdom of God and the New Testament strategies with a basketful of disconnected tactics.

Consider the radical Islamic fundamentalists. They seem to separate tactics from their goal and strategies better than the United States government. If this were not true we would be fighting a war against Islamic *world domination* (the real issue) instead of a "War on Terror." Terror is a tactic used in support of strategies aimed toward a single goal. If the church is to establish the kingdom of God, we must distinguish the tactics from the strategies from the overarching goal.

Keep the Goal in Mind

If the New Testament calls out a _goal_ of a worldwide kingdom of God through individual conversions, then the strategies we seek ought to come from the same document. We should look first to Jesus for strategies.

If we keep the kingdom of God uppermost, the New Testament reads differently than if we subjugate it to a manual for personal holiness. Instead of merely functioning as a devotional guide, it becomes a handbook for revolution. Oh, we will grow spiritually as we read it. In fact, if we read the New Testament as a manual for revolution, our own personal walk with God will accelerate far beyond what we would glean if we only read it for comforting thoughts.

Jesus called Peter and Andrew to mission over devotion when He said, "Follow Me, and I will make you fishers of men" (Matt. 4:19, _NKJV_). The call to discipleship is a call to mission. Personal piety is part of the package. It was not, and is not, the end goal. Discipling the nations is. If the goal is to bring the nations into commitment to Jesus Christ, how should we approach the task? The answer is pretty clear: "What Would Jesus Do?" especially if you can stretch your brain enough to see Jesus as the first church planter—the one Paul emulated.

Now, give me a little break here—I know that "What Would Jesus Do?" has long been cliché. But the problem with clichés is that they are truisms we ignore to our detriment. We cannot afford to bypass this one. We know what Jesus would do, because we know what He _did_. We know, not just what He would do to a wounded Samaritan, but what He would do if He were trying to start a spiritual revolution. Our problem is that we seldom "go and do likewise." Let's take another look at "What Would Jesus Do?" and see if it can't show us the way to an overarching strategy in support of the GOAL.

Jesus and Multiplication

Jesus communicated the gospel widely while simultaneously working closely with a few people. Jesus eventually chose 12 personal disciples. You could even say He operated a portable seminary as He poured Himself into these people. Moreover, He drew an inner circle of three men who learned things the others didn't.

Jesus duplicated Himself in His disciples and gave them His authority to do the things He did. This came to a high climax when He was able to send 72 people on a mission to bless other towns, heal the sick and proclaim that the kingdom of God had come to them. They were also to pray that the Lord would raise up others to do the same thing because the harvest is great and the workers are few (see Luke 10:2). If you follow the progression recorded in Luke, you find Jesus modeling evangelism to the 12, plus a few women who traveled with them (see Luke 8:1-4). He then deputizes those 12 to a similar mission (see Luke 9:1-6). Finally, He commissions 72 to a ministry trip quite similar to that of the 12 (see Luke 10:1-16). Each mission looks like the one before it. The first sets the mark for the other two. The third suggests that the second bore fruit in an expanded number of leaders. The whole thing is about multiplying leaders as much as followers.

Jesus was so serious about calling men and women to His kingdom that His disciples were to actually pronounce judgment on those who refused their message—hardly a seeker-sensitive approach (see Luke 10:1-16). Later, He gave them instructions to bring *all* the nations into obedience to Him (see Matt. 28:18-20). Their (and our) task is nothing short of worldwide revolution.

Do you find it remarkable that these 72 people had learned so much of Jesus and His authority that they returned saying, "Lord, even the demons obey us when we use your name" (Luke 10:17)? This was a growth situation, both numerically and experientially. And do you fully embrace the implications of His directive when He told these 72 people, "The harvest is great, but the workers are few. So pray to the Lord who is in charge of the harvest; ask him to send more workers for his fields" (Luke 10:2)? The Scripture never records Jesus commissioning more than those 72 to direct mission. But he didn't stop at 72. The call to pray for labor suggests an ever-growing army of mission-capable leaders.

Jesus began with a small group. He duplicated His knowledge, experience and power in that handful of people. Apparently, they did the same. This isn't gospel, but if you separate Peter, James and John from the rest of the disciples, you could send them back in as group leaders of three disciples each, each unit a microcosm of the 12. This "small-small" group strategy is new to the modern church. Church planter and founder of Church Multiplication Associates, Neil Cole, does an outstanding job of bringing it alive in his book *Cultivating a Harvest for God*.

I know that I risk over-emphasizing a point. But I believe that Peter, James and John understood that if Jesus had three close disciples, they should as well. My question is, "Do you?" And, "Do your disciples each have two or three?" Therein lies the key to whatever success I've enjoyed as a multiplier of churches. Our church-planting success stems directly from close relationships between myself and a few "disciples." But it doesn't stop there. My disciples each have a close circle of disciples, and so on. This discipleship pyramid occasionally falters about four levels down, but toward the top it has been very productive as a training tool for prospective church multipliers.

This concept of relationally multiplying leadership is a foundational element in Jesus' example to us. You may disagree with me over Peter, James and John being "sub-leaders" within the 12. But *however* the 12 learned to operate, by the time we get to Luke 10, there were 72 committed and well-trained disciples commissioned to minister and pray for others to join their ranks.

10

POSSIBILITY

· · · · · · · · · · · · · · · · · · · ·

DOING WHAT
JESUS DID

When we talk of strategy, we are looking for a few simple principles that will stand the test of time. Just as there are battle strategies of the ancient Romans or the Mongols that are in use today, we need to look for basic operational principles in Jesus' life that He would have handed over to His disciples before telling them to take the nations back from the devil.

Jesus' stated mission was, "I will build my church, and all the powers of hell will not conquer it" (Matt. 16:18). His strategy was to empower a few people who would empower others to change the world. In the same passage, He promises, "I will give you the keys of the Kingdom of Heaven. Whatever you lock on earth will be locked in heaven, and whatever you open on earth will be opened in heaven" (Matt. 16:19). The terminology of keys and locks suggest the power to guide, through prayer, to open and close situations, as we ask.

Keys of the Kingdom of Heaven

The Church, or "called out ones," are given these keys to the kingdom of heaven in order to pass them on to others until the powers of darkness are broken down. I can identify five such keys.

Key 1: Accept Your Calling

Jesus had to accept His own calling. The 40 days of temptation in the wilderness was a direct challenge to that calling.
His call was to declare the Kingdom, die to pay the penalty
for our sins, rise from the dead, send the Holy Spirit to empower His disciples and then reign over the nations. Satan
promised Him creature comforts and a shortcut to rule over
"the nations of the world and all their glory" (Matt. 4:8).
A simple, self-serving act would have produced a "kingdom." But it would have fallen far short of what the Father
had in mind.

Every leader among us faces the same temptation. Will
we settle for comfort and a prize short of the goal? Is personal peace and safety our primary concern? If so, we will
opt out for the fortress-like security of our churches with
little actual sense of God's kingdom on earth. Do we seek
significance in the eyes of people? That sets us up for
church as a reflection of our ego—the bigger the better. It is
natural to desire regard as visible, reputable members of our
communities. Respect is a big deal. But it can so easily lead
to the counterfeit goal of building our own kingdom.

One question we all face is, "Am I willing to accept the
Great Commission as a personal calling?" If the answer is
yes, then nothing will stand between us and spiritual revolution. Our gifts of time, money and prestige will burst with
sacrifice. You and I will crave the power of the Holy Spirit so
that we can make a difference wherever we go. If we embrace
the goal of spiritual revolution, we will only be happy in a
church that sees itself as a *force for change* and acts accordingly. It will be easy to set aside comfortable tradition (even
the tradition of the last decade) for functional steps toward
the goal of Christ's kingdom realized in our generation.

The point is that, like Peter and Andrew, you and I must be willing to become "fishers of men" on a much broader scale. We simply need more fishing boats.

Key 2: Recruit by Revelation

I think we often miss the prayer element in Jesus' strategy. I think He had already prayed to the Lord of the Harvest for workers before He ever told Peter and Andrew, "Follow me, and I will make you fishers of men" (Matt. 4:19, *KJV*).

This whole deal hinges on the power of the Holy Spirit that was in Jesus since the day of His baptism. Remember, He became fully human in Bethlehem. When the Holy Spirit descended upon Him, He received power to witness of the father like that which He promised us in Acts 1:8. He called a few trusting and trustworthy people and communicated that power to them along with a new worldview. It stands to reason that He would have prayed for laborers before calling them— especially since He told them to do the same. His strategy starts with prayer for ministry partners.

After praying, Jesus called those whom the Lord revealed to Him. Remember how He was able to tell Nathaniel that he was a good man and that He had seen him sitting under a fig tree before Philip called him (see John 1:37-49)? Are you looking for revelation when you call people to serve? Or do you recruit just to manage the church? Jesus pulled people into His inner circle at the direction of the Holy Spirit and in answer to His prayers.

He lived according to divine revelation so much that He could say, "I assure you, the Son can do nothing by himself. He does only what he sees the Father doing. Whatever the Father does, the Son also does. For the Father loves the Son and tells him everything he is doing" (John 5:19-20). Calling a few people as directed by the Father is the second ingredient in Jesus' strategy.

Key 3: Communicate Broadly with Holy Spirit Power

The third element in Jesus' strategy—a broad communication with many people—probably works concurrently with the first two. Jesus spread His message to all who would listen. We would be foolish if we overlooked the fact that He not only *preached* that the kingdom of God was near, but He also *demonstrated* it. The miracles of Jesus were the ticket into the hearts of those who heard Him. Even Peter was immediately convicted of sin when he pulled that first gigantic net full of fish into his boat. His response to that miracle was to fall on his knees and say, "Oh, Lord, please leave me—I'm too much of a sinner to be around you" (Luke 5:8). The miracle brought his spiritual need to the surface of his heart.

It was after Peter confessed spiritual poverty that Jesus invited him to come fish for men. We often fail to connect the dots here: Peter experienced a miracle that revealed to him his own sinful heart. It is after this revelation that he was called into ministry. To separate these events is to miss the role of the miraculous in evangelism and discipleship. Unfortunately, in the West we've separated the miraculous (if we acknowledge it at all) from discipleship, evangelism and world mission.

It is interesting to me that in Luke 10, Jesus told the 72 to "heal the sick" before He told them to announce the Kingdom. I wonder what would happen if we taught our disciples to pray with pre-Christians before preaching to them?

A good friend of mine grew up believing that miracles ceased with the death of the last apostle. He currently serves as an underground church planter operating in several Islamic nations. He and his teams have planted several thousand hidden churches. He now talks about miracles on a daily basis. I recently asked him about his changed paradigm. His response was, "You can't do effective ministry among Moslems without becoming a Pentecostal." Actually, he is not a Pentecostal by affiliation. What he meant is that you can't survive, nor effectively evangelize, without power encounters with the Holy Spirit. It is the power of God in everyday situations that rolls back darkness in a culture bent on killing anyone who converts to Christ. We won't establish Christ's kingdom without the supernatural.

We should note that miracles did not end with Jesus or the apostles. The apostles and their inheritors rode into prominence on the back of power over demonic forces plaguing the Roman Empire. As late as the seventh century, we read of Pope Gregory warning an English bishop against pride over the conversion of local leaders through miracles of healing.[1] The wonders of the post-apostolic Christians destroyed belief in heathen gods while they enlisted allegiance to Christ's kingdom.[2] Entire cultures embraced Christ because the kingdom of heaven invaded physical reality in the healing of broken minds and bodies.

Supernatural works were so tied in to Jesus' message that some people focused on the material results of these miracles and missed the spiritual truth altogether. Jesus rebuked this attitude on the day after feeding the five thousand: "The truth is, you want to be with me because I fed you, not because you saw the miraculous sign" (John 6:26). These people not only missed His message, but they skipped over the significance of the miracle because they were excited about a free lunch. When He later told them that He was the bread of life and that they had to eat His flesh, many forsook Him, leaving Him with those who had spiritual eyes and ears (see John 6:25-71).

We need to go in the power of the Spirit. And our message must be one of power rather than just good advice.

Key 4: Make Disciples

Jesus protected His time by investing attention that others longed for in just a few well-chosen people (see Matt. 8:18). He apparently used life's everyday situations to teach them, even using their fears for instruction in faith (see Matt. 8:23-27). He privately explained His parables to them (see Matt. 13:10-11). Jesus revealed Himself to the inner circle of Peter, James and John in ways the world never saw (see Luke 9:28-36). The gospels spill more ink describing personal discipleship than they do on Jesus' time with crowds.

He mentored His followers so deeply that we have turned the English noun "disciple," or "learner," into a verb. Because of Jesus' strong example, we now say that He "discipled" those who were closest to Him. To disciple someone is different from mentoring them. A mentor watches and coaches; a discipler teaches someone to adhere to an existing standard. Jesus did not say that we should mentor the nations, but that we should "Teach these new disciples to obey all the commands I have given you" (Matt. 28:20).

This doesn't require adherence to static traditions and rituals. It does assume a baseline. You must learn to imitate before you gain real power to innovate.

Key 5: Commission and Empower Your Disciples

Jesus called and trained ordinary men. They were fishermen, farmers and a tax collector. Even after the apostles healed a lame man in Jerusalem, the authorities saw them as perhaps lower-class people. They deemed them "unlearned and ignorant men," yet they marveled at their actions and "took knowledge of them that they had been with Jesus" (Acts 4:13, *KJV*).

Between Jesus' crucifixion and the day they healed the blind man, two significant things happened to Peter and John. Jesus formally commissioned them and the other apostles to an implacable goal. Then He empowered them when He baptized them in His Holy Spirit. By Pentecost afternoon, they began to understand both their task and the power that could catapult them to success.

Giving someone a task and telling them that you believe in them is powerful medicine. When Jesus laid the goal of world conquest on His disciples, He immediately elevated them to a role of partnership with Himself. No longer just disciples, they were now apostles—"sent out ones." They were on a mission from God and they knew they were unstoppable.

After Pentecost, they no longer acted like unlearned and ignorant fishermen. They faced down the world and its authorities with the grace and power of God. They would turn a major portion of the world upside down in their lifetime. They knew the Lord, embraced the goal and understood the power they possessed. They were ready to replicate Jesus' strategy to the ends of the earth.

We toss around words like "empower" without much spiritual thought. To us the term generally means to loose the bonds of regulations allowing freedom to make meaningful decisions. Good try but no cigar. We must find ways to bring spiritual power into the lives of those we commission. The very idea of laying on of hands has degraded into a ritual of endorsement, when it began as a bestowal of spiritual gifts.

We see the results of impartation in Stephen (see Acts 6:8), Philip (see Acts 8:1-13) and Peter and John (see Acts 8:14-16). And Paul's assumptions in 1 Corinthians 12–14 center on the enduring nature of Holy Spirit power in the church.

An Apostolic Force

The goal is to bring the entire world into reverence of Christ and make disciples of whole nations. Keeping focus on the goal, we can activate all five elements of this strategy including the impartation of power to our own disciples. But it will all be meaningless if church leaders (you and me) only maintain a defensive posture. Our calling is to disciple the nations of this world. It was and is an "apostolic mission."

There is too much ado about the meaning of the word "apostle." Many maintain that it applies only to the 11 loyal disciples plus Paul. However, the New Testament attaches the title to others such as Barnabas (see Acts 4:36; 14:14) or Andronicus and Junias (see Rom. 16:7).

My point here is that the word "apostle" means a delegate, an ambassador or, literally, "one who is sent." Disciples may remain at home learning—they fit in both a church as a *fortress* and a church as a mission *field*. Apostles are on the move. They only work well in a church that sees itself as a *force* to win the nations to Christ. Disciples can function in a defensive posture while apostles must be on the offensive by nature of their calling. If we accept the goal, we all become apostles no matter where we live or work.

Goals, Strategies and Tactics

After identifying the goal and a strategy, we can begin to look for *tactics* that might work best in our situation. I want to be careful to say here that the Bible gives us what I call "true-truth." To me this means that whatever I read is historically and spiritually accurate. If I separate ancient Hebrew culture from the events, I discover truths that affect any culture at any time in history. As a result, I strongly disapprove of calling the New Testament Christians "the *primitive* church." I believe they were more like "the *prototype* for church." In other words, what they did and said are true and useful for all time.

However, I do *not* believe that the Bible sets out to display what I would call "all-truth." Do we read of every miracle that Jesus did? No! John said that such a record would fill all the books in the world (see John 20:30; 21:25). Do we know the names of those people who traveled from Cyprus and Cyrene to plant the church at Antioch? We not only don't know their names, but we also know almost nothing of their methodology (see Acts 11:19-20). At this level, we are dealing in *tactics*. The goal never changes. The strategy is a constant. But the tactics can and should change according to the situation. However, a good baseline for tactics is found in the gospels and in the Acts of the Apostles. We will start from there.

11

FAILURE AND SUCCESS

• •

MULTIPLICATION IN THE EARLY CHURCH

It was persecution that drove the first church planters out of Jerusalem. And we must take note: The first church planters were not the apostles trained by Jesus. The first recorded instance of the church taking the gospel outside of Jerusalem is in Acts 8, where we read "and all the believers except the apostles fled into Judea and Samaria" (v. 1). The text describes Philip's success in that city. The persecution wasn't necessary to the multiplication of the church, but it did set in motion some ideas that became endemic to the movement as multiplication later became intentional.

I read Acts on a daily basis. I simply read whatever chapter corresponds to the date. I do the same with a different gospel each month. Admittedly, my reading pattern is abbreviated whenever I am in Mark, but you get the idea. I figure that if I am going to do church, I should learn from the masters.

Reluctant Apostles

Each time I read the book of Acts, I am freshly disappointed by the apostles. Although I already know what they didn't do,

I continue to have my hopes dashed by the words, "all the believers *except* the apostles fled into Judea and Samaria" (Acts 8:1, emphasis added). Those guys were told to await the promise of the Father (see Luke 24:49) . . . *not* to hang around town until the second coming!

They certainly displayed courage staying in Jerusalem with Saul of Tarsus hot on their tails. But they were hardly trotting off to the uttermost parts of the earth as instructed. These guys were courageously disobedient. And, unfortunately, they have become examples worthy of imitation down through the centuries. Ask the average prominent church leader if he or she would consider moving overseas to launch a movement and see what kind of an answer you get.

I'm not suggesting that everyone should drop everything and buy airplane tickets. But I do want you to notice that the nine years between Acts chapters 1 and 8 were more than enough time for the 12 to pack their bags and buy tickets on a boat or a camel caravan. Please note that it was only *after* Philip had success in Samaria that Peter and John ventured out of Judea. Following their extraordinary ministry in Samaria, the Holy Spirit still had to pop a miracle to get Peter into Cornelius' living room (see Acts 10). It breaks my heart that by the time Peter hooked up with Gentiles, Saul was already preaching Jesus, to the dismay of the Jews in Damascus. Where were these guys' heads?

Have you ever noticed that the Twelve appear only in the first chapter of Acts? James is named in two chapters. John gets notice in three. And Peter shows up in only 11 (with one of those a full repeat of the previous chapter because the other apostles are skeptical of his mission to the Gentiles)—so much for his role as the first pope. Did it ever cross your mind that Saul/Paul shows up in 21 chapters of a book titled "Acts of the

Apostles," while midway through the book the original apostles are still busy holding council in Jerusalem? This stuff drives me insane. How is it so easy to set up camp while ignoring the simple command "Go"?

For some reason, the Twelve just never seemed to get it. Paul did, and that's why so many trees gave their lives to recounting his deeds.

Unnamed Christians

Alongside of Paul, there are the exploits of some unnamed Christians—apostles by default. The Holy Spirit through Luke describes them, "The believers who had fled Jerusalem went everywhere preaching the Good News about Jesus" (Acts 8:4). Then he gives us a for instance: "Philip, for example . . ." (v. 5). In other words, Philip's experience was just one of many. These unnamed apostles effectively spread the word across the Mediterranean world in ways much similar to Philip in Samaria.

If the organized church wouldn't get the job done, God would turn to the disorganized church. That fleeing group of refugees was probably without great financial resources, because most refugees are as tattered as they are scattered. But they stayed on mission.

The goal of the kingdom of God must have never been far from their minds. I love the story as we pick it up later in Acts 11:19: "Meanwhile, the believers who had fled from Jerusalem during the persecution after Stephen's death traveled as far as Phoenicia, Cyprus and Antioch of Syria." Some transplanted fairly close to home. Others acted as an invasion force on an offshore island. Still others went to another country more than 350 miles away. Jesus' invasion plan was finally in operation.

Better yet, while the early arrivers in Antioch preached to Jews only, some of the later immigrants stepped over the racial barrier to preach to Gentiles. Now the clash of kingdoms functioned on multinational and multiethnic fronts. Those believers from Cyprus and Cyrene (modern Libya) "began preaching to Gentiles . . . the power of the Lord was upon them, and large numbers of these Gentiles believed and turned to the Lord" (Acts 11:20-21). These unnamed apostles launched a multiethnic church in Antioch, a Gentile city.

To Give a Blessing or Not?

Of course, the institutional church always faces a choice: to give its blessing or break up the rabble. Apparently due to Peter's experience in Caesarea, they were able to send Barnabas with authority to bless what God was already blessing, and a powerful church was born.

It was this church that would become the primary launch point for missionary raids throughout the Mediterranean and southern Europe. It was from Antioch, not Jerusalem, that Jesus' strategies took the shape of men and material. It was from Antioch that the Great Commission began to look like reality.

The failure of the Jerusalem church to mobilize threatened the worldwide growth of the Kingdom. No one knows for certain why the original apostles chose to remain in Jerusalem. We do know that by staying they failed to live out the command to "go." Their sterility jeopardized the entire mission. Without the folks in Antioch, the church would never have survived, much less conquered Rome. This tale of two cities is pregnant with a message for you and me.

12

METHODS

· ·

WHAT WOULD
PAUL DO?

What about Paul? Was he strategic or did he just throw spit wads against a wall, hoping that some would stick?

Of course, we would say that he was strategic in his approach—or at least led by the Spirit. We see wisdom in Barnabas and Saul, two Jews from pagan lands, launching ministry to Jews living in pagan lands. Their first preaching attempt in Cyprus, Barnabas' home turf, accentuates their tactics. Later, we see Paul forbidden by the Spirit from entering Asia Minor (see Acts 16:6); but on his next mission, he enjoyed such great success that "all who lived in Asia heard the word of the Lord" (Acts 19:10, *NASB*). At this point, Paul was on his home turf since he grew up nearby.

So, there is a strategy to be discerned from Paul. And we might possibly make more use of him as a *model* than even Jesus. The reason for this is that Paul was human and not the Son of God. We have a better chance of emulating him than Jesus—at least in our own minds. My purpose here is to "humanize" the task, making it attainable for "ordinary men who had had no special training" (Acts 4:13). I'd also like to pull together essentials rather than every detail of Paul's life. Again, we need to separate tactics from strategies and the goal of the worldwide kingdom of God.

Strategy vs. Tactics

When we elevate tactics to a strategic level, we major in minors. Here again, the lessons of 1943 are useful to us. The Allied goal was twofold: control Berlin and destroy the enemy's will to make war. The strategy was fairly straightforward: (1) deny the enemy the resources of the Middle East, (2) destroy the industrial might of the Nazi war machine by air raids, and (3) funnel enough men and material through Normandy to win what had become a three-front war.

The tactics included construction of amphibious landing craft, the use of specially constructed tanks to cut through the hedgerows of Northern France and inventing plywood gliders to launch a first-strike team into key positions. We could talk of ships used as artillery positions, or the Normandy invasion that saw the first truly successful use of airborne soldiers or paratroopers. And Ike's network of spies is the stuff of legend. All of these and thousands of other examples are only tactics. None was absolutely necessary to the cause. Each would bow to the essential strategy for winning the war. Fall in love with tactics and you threaten strategy. Let strategy dominate and tactics usually show themselves useful or not. Need I remind you of the danger of copying tactics learned at the last conference or seminar you attended?

Paul's Goal and Strategy

For Paul, the goal was to bring the entire world into reverence of Christ, to make disciples of whole nations. I like to think that he understood that his role was that of establishing a bridgehead over which others would cross.

His strategy was the same as that of Jesus. He put shoe leather under the lessons of the Gospels. That is why he is mentioned in 21 of the 28 chapters in the Acts of the Apostles. He is the central actor in the drama of early church multi-plication. He was acting out the life message of Jesus.

The strategy in Paul's life is pretty much the same as what we saw in Jesus' (at least according to me): (1) accept your call-ing, (2) recruit by revelation, (3) communicate broadly with Holy Spirit power, (4) make disciples, and (5) commission and empower your disciples.

Accept Your Calling

Put yourself in Paul's boots. You've been feared and largely re-jected by the church in Jerusalem. Almost by default, you are introduced to a lively congregation where God is obviously work-ing. You emerge somewhere near the top of the heap as a leader. One day you and your friends are fasting and praying. You prob-ably expect a stronger move of the Spirit in your church. But the Holy Spirit throws you a curveball. He calls you away from all this love and security to multiply churches in a hostile world that knows next to nothing about someone named "Jesus" from a dusty village in Palestine called Nazareth.

It's enough to break your heart. I know, because it happened to me. I was happily pastoring a large church in a Southern Cal-ifornia beach town when the Spirit called me to start over in a small town on the rainy backside of Oahu. It turned out to be the best break of my life. But when it happened, it felt like I was giv-ing up security for oblivion.

Knowing and accepting your calling is powerful; so what else is new? But, I question whether the current stasis in the church isn't indicative that some who may be called away from apparent success into the great unknown might be sitting around the fire warming their hands. Why else hasn't the church in America grown numerically in the past 20 years? Why is church multipli-cation not keeping up with population growth?

Recruit by Revelation

Jesus recruited by revelation. We see it in the Gospels. Frankly, I see no evidence of this in Paul's life as recorded in Acts or the epistles unless you stretch his words to Timothy about the "laying on of hands" to include revelation that Paul experienced—I don't. This is the single indicator of strategy that seems to differ from Jesus'.

There are no stories of recruitment dreams paralleling the one involving the man from Macedonia. Nor does Paul claim visions of righteous men sitting under trees, as Jesus did. Other than the initial calling at the prayer meeting in Antioch, his choice of companions seems to have been a matter of convenience. John Mark went along as a helper. After breaking with Barnabas over Mark, Paul took up with Silas who had made the trip with him back from the Jerusalem Council. Later, he adds Timothy to his missionary band pretty much at the recommendation of the folks at Lystra and Iconium. Luke, Erastus, Sopater, Aristarchus, Secundus, Gaius, Tychicus and Trophimus are also mentioned as Paul's companions. But there is no mention of divine revelation associated with their call. *Interesting*

I actually find this comforting. I believe in calling by revelation. It has happened in my own life and in relation to others I've discipled. But my experience shows it can be the exception rather than the norm. I am always alert for people who have followers. This is the strongest indication of leadership that we have. A leader is simply a person who has a follower. They may be a bad leader or a good one. Maybe rebellious. Maybe confused or even a heretic.

I simply make it my business to get to know the leaders around me. Sometimes I do get a little shot from the Spirit that an individual has something going on between him and

God that I should get into. But mostly I am looking for people who can lead and are willing to step up to the high task of multiplying the church.

Communicate Broadly with Holy Spirit Power

This is a tough call for many Western Christians. We find ourselves marginalized by a society that has consigned our message to the rubbish heap of obsolescence. We are even further marginalized by our own equivocation over the power of the Spirit.

We waver between misgivings about the miraculous and the faith that God can heal today (usually depending on whether the illness is personal or not). My own background is that of a classic Pentecostal church. But, if we are honest with ourselves, we will admit that much of our theology has reduced itself to mere theory. We, like many of our more conservative brethren, believe in miracles—a long time ago in a faraway place. Somehow, wedding God's power to our message is a problem.

The difficulty with that problem is that it leaves us moralizing instead of liberating. We preach good advice instead of transformation. We've come too far from the early Christian view that Jesus "chose fishermen, artisans, rustics, and unskilled persons . . . that they being sent through various nations should perform all those miracles without any deceit and without any material aids."[1]

Now, I'm not trying to make a Pentecostal out of you or anyone else. I am contending that the touch of the supernatural accompanied the evangelistic efforts of Paul like it did that of Jesus and His original disciples. Even a casual reading of the Acts of the Apostles will convince you that Paul believed Jesus' words to "heal the sick [and] as you heal them, say, 'The Kingdom of God is near you now'" (Luke 10:9).

How did this translate into reality in Paul's life? Well, the people of Lystra thought Barnabas was Jupiter and Paul was Mercury because they had healed a lame man (see Acts 14:12). Or what about the hot water they got into over the demonized slave girl in Philippi? Better yet, what do you make of the conversion of the jailer after their praise songs triggered an earthquake (see Acts 16:16-40)? Paul was able to evangelize the people of Malta after surviving a poisonous reptile bite and healing the father of Publius, the chief official of the island (see Acts 28:1-10). Paul's preaching was in partnership with the Spirit's supernatural work.

At home, we try to teach our people to pray first and preach later. We've found that almost anyone is open to prayer. Even fairly anti-Christian people respond positively to an offer for prayer—often with tears in their eyes. Our experience is that evangelism isn't so hard if someone has experienced God's love in the shape of an answered prayer.

We are good at broadly communicating the gospel. We are getting better at communicating the Spirit's power. But in my experience, we have yet to link the two in a meaningful way. It is worth noting that every spiritual awakening in living memory seemed to link these two functions as a single strategy.

Make Disciples

Paul made disciples wherever he preached. We know this because he was able to appoint some of those disciples as elders when he moved on. It wasn't enough to make converts and move on like we do through media ministries or even as happens in large-event evangelism.

This is perhaps best illustrated in Acts 14, where Paul preached *and* made many disciples in Derbe, only to return to his last three cities, strengthening the believers there. We don't know exactly how he made disciples. Because technology was limited, whatever he did involved face-to-face communication. He had no access to email, a website, printing press or even a bicycle. The very lack of information given in Acts suggests that Luke assumed we would understand this process from his recording of it in his earlier writing, the Gospel. You find the person of peace and hang out!

However you shake it, a major strategy for Paul involved making disciples, be it Silas and Timothy or John Mark, whom he would later describe as "useful to me for service" (2 Tim. 4:11, *NASB*). Had I asked Paul, "Can you name the Peter, James and John in your life?" I am certain he would tick off a list of names without catching his breath. But here's the deal: What would you say if I asked you the same question?

Commission and Empower Your Disciples

The mention of disciples in Lystra bridges into Paul's strengthening the believers in Lystra, Iconium and Antioch of Pisidia. The text goes on to reveal the fifth leg of Paul's strategy: "Paul and Barnabas also appointed elders in every church and prayed for them with fasting, turning them over to the care of the Lord, in whom they had come to trust" (Acts 14:23). Paul and Barnabas were not just itinerant preachers. They were itinerant church planters. They multiplied the church in nearly every city they touched.

The process of appointing elders, along with fasting and prayer, culminates in "turning them over to the care of the Lord, in whom they had come to trust." That last phrase probably refers to the fact that these new elders had learned to trust in the Lord. It also underscores the trust that Barnabas and Paul had in the Lord. They had no time for thorough training. They had no seminaries. There was no denominational structure to hold these new pastors (and congregations) together. Their whole deal was built on relationships.

Trust in the Lord, Not Tactics

Trust in the Lord was a big deal to these pioneer church multipliers . . . perhaps a bigger deal than it is to us today. And here is the main thrust of this book: do you think it is possible that we would multiply churches, and disciples, faster if we trusted more in the Lord and less in our tactics?

On a macro scale, today's Church in the West implements the first four elements of Jesus' and Paul's strategy with a fair amount of intentionality. It is the fifth element where we get our wheels stuck in the mud, probably due to the roadblocks mentioned earlier. We work our programs (tactics) with some degree of success—at least enough success to make us feel good about ourselves, even enough to gather some notoriety and influence. Yet the Kingdom goal goes unmet. We are not discipling our own nation, let alone all the nations. We still have plenty to learn from Paul.

SLOGANS

. . . .

STATEMENTS OF MISSION AND PURPOSE

We tend to forget the very implications of the word "church." We are the "called out of God." But called out for what purpose? Jesus said that we should bear much fruit and that our fruit should remain (see John 15:5,16). He clearly set the bar by instructing us to make disciples of the nations. Paul shows us the way by multiplying converts, disciples and churches.

Confronting the Misery Index

The *ecclesia* is called to change the world—your church and mine. Our people should affect the culture around them. I remember a presidential election debate when Ronald Reagan held the presidency of Jimmy Carter up to a standard he called the "misery index." The thing was simple. He asked the American people if they were better off or worse off after four years under Carter. Apparently, they felt that the misery index climbed under Carter, because they elected Reagan.

That index might be a useful measure of a church. You could ask, "Is our community more or less miserable because of how we live our lives?" Such a standard might be a better indicator of church health than numbers, budget or even evangelism numbers.

I just returned from Nepal where pastors teach church members how to start businesses. These guys are seriously denting their own misery index. On the same trip, I traveled to Myanmar eight days after the storm that destroyed 30 percent of the rice fields and killed more than 100,000 people. One church overseer could count more than 8,000 members dead. The churches there are poor and persecuted. It is taking outside help in the form of friendship and money to enable those Christians to address the needs around them.

The Effective Twelve

Jesus' disciples, the original "called-out ones," made a difference in the misery index in their world. They brought spiritual power to bear on the misery around them. They moved into new territory, filled with confidence in God's power to alleviate misery. They roughly approximated the mission He defined in Luke 4 when He announced His ministry.

Pressing the battle into the streets and sickrooms, they prayed their way into the hearts of lost souls. They were so effective that when they returned from their mission, Jesus said He saw Satan fall like lightning from heaven (see Luke 10:18). I find it quite interesting that He immediately told them to remain "unexcited" about their power over the devil but to rejoice that their names were written in heaven.

So what was that all about? Why didn't Jesus throw a party to celebrate with them? I'd have been back-slapping and high-fiving these guys until the sun went down. They apparently healed broken bodies and exorcized demons using Jesus' name. How could they not be excited? Why tell them to cool their jets? What was Jesus' point?

I used to think of His words as some sort of put-down on the miraculous or an indication that the age of miracles would soon end. But the past 50 years have shown that miracles are still part of the program—say, in places like China or Latin America, where the Church truly invades the darkness. I think Jesus was simply briefing His forces once again on their larger mission. Their names were written in heaven and it was their job to see many more entries in heaven's database. Prayer, healing, exorcism and so on are powerful tactics and useful in the contest, but they ultimately only represent skirmishes, not the war.

The Church is called to *reproduce* itself. Our task is to overwhelm the enemy in ever-growing numbers. Bringing miracles to unchurched people is a first step. Bringing people to Christ is taking back ground on the battlefield. But the big issue remains the spiritual conquest of nations and the spirits that rule them. When this army of love called the Church occupies territory previously held by the enemy, the misery indicator drops accordingly.

None would disagree that we all could use more of the Spirit's power. But many fail to see that everywhere that power is mentioned or recommended in Acts, it is in the context of world mission. We are called to disciple nations, a task that will only be accomplished by multiplying churches. It's not enough to establish the beachhead; we must control the field.

A Statement of Purpose

Strategy is important. Stating it clearly, what we call church strategy often just clones the latest craze. While most of these trends are useful, I find some of them perplexing.

A few years ago, it seemed that *the* key to church growth would be a carefully crafted "mission statement" or a "statement of purpose" (these are not synonyms—they are different). Tom Peters promoted a statement of purpose in his classic business book *In Search of Excellence*. That may be the reason the book sold so well. It took the focus of business off of bean counting and put it back on fundamental values. Similarly, Jim Collins, in his book *Good to Great,* underscores the value of mission statements. Both books are worth reading, and each author is right—you need to spell out your mission in the most basic terms possible if you hope to achieve very much.

Because of these books and others like them, there was a blitz of statements popping up on church websites across the country. Most were biblical, but some were not. Many were succinct, but most were terribly wordy. A few were apparently supposed to be cool, or even funny. In some cases, too much creativity voided the effort, as did wordiness. While the majority reflected Jesus' *statement of mission*, the Great Commission, nearly all of them missed the one *statement of purpose* clearly recorded in the New Testament.

You ask, "If our mission is to disciple nations, then isn't that the same thing as our purpose?" I suppose you could say so. However, I think purpose is different from mission. Purpose submits to mission but is necessarily different from it. Think back to World War II. The mission was to break the will of the Germans. The purpose was to build a military force capable of attaining the mission.

I think Paul makes this strategic point when he defines the purpose for leaders in *every* congregation. He writes that Jesus gave church leaders "for the equipping of the saints for the work of ministry" (Eph. 4:12, *NKJV*). The operating word in that phrase is "for." It delineates the purpose of leadership in the local church. The purpose of these five classes of leaders is to *equip* God's people to do His work. If every leader has the same purpose, wouldn't you think the overall church purpose should line up with it? Your church exists to equip your members to do God's work—both on and off campus.

Many of us describe our purpose in terms of serving our people. We've set the bar too low. We'll serve them on the way to equipping them. Or, we say our purpose is evangelism. Again, only part of the equation. Some describe their church as existing to better the community—nice down payment, but no prize. The world is our mission, and we must equip our people toward that goal.

Notice the general change in direction here. If I intend to evangelize, serve or entertain, the structures I build will generally move people inward toward our church campus. As soon as I redefine my purpose and that of our congregation in terms of equipping, I point our people outward. Outward to where? The ends of the earth. And I've discovered that the thing is round. The ends of the earth only exist in my mind. When we point outward, we can just keep going. When you pass "Go," you discover that there is still more earth to reach.

There are no boundaries for a church with an outward focus and an equipping purpose. You become a local church with a global mission. My friend Carol Davis calls such a congregation a "Global-Local church."

If you don't focus on equipping, you can still touch the world by giving to missions, hiring church planters and so on. But your impact will be limited, like, perhaps Iceland's during World War II—contributing to the cause, but in a limited way.

Change your purpose to equipping and you can't help but put boots on the ground. You help smother the world with the liberating good news that Jesus came to set captives free, preach good news to the poor and restore sight to the blind. An equipping church leads every member to live as a missionary, at home and on the road, in God's great invasion force.

14

VISION

. . . .

WHAT SHAPES
THE NEW CHURCH?

So, we've got mission and we've got purpose. What about structure? I got into a great discussion with a friend who plants house churches. He was going off about terminology. It seems he could no longer stomach the phrase "cell church," and he has a problem with that other pesky term, "mega-church." To him, every church should be defined in the first 10 verses of Luke 10. In other words, he thinks we all belong in house churches led by volunteers.

I agree with his sentiments, but not his conclusions. House churches equip leaders quickly. They multiply rapidly. And real estate isn't usually a problem. But I am not ready to run around the country padlocking church buildings in the name of progress. You can imagine that our discussion soon morphed into a colorful debate.

We were rescued by a friend, who put it this way: "Look, one of you is a Luke 10 pastor and the other is an Acts 2 pastor. So accept each other and get over it!" What my friend meant was that we have each built our churches around a different passage of Scripture describing the logistics of God working among His people. I guess each of us could have responded, "At least we're building on the Bible rather than the traditions of men." But he had a point; we *both* limit God in our narrow focus.

Now, I doubt you'll be able to find many form and function working models for *ecclesia* anywhere in the Bible other than in those two passages (you certainly won't find one in the Old Testament). Nor do I think you need to. In fact, I would imagine anyone reading this would identify with one or both of these church models: the cell church of Acts 2 or the simple church described in Luke 10.

However you see your church, I have three questions for you: (1) Does your church include the multiplication factor described in each of these Scriptures? (2) Could you visualize Luke 10 as a starting point for an Acts 2 church? (3) Do you see church multiplication as the most natural method for fulfilling the Great Commission?

The Luke 10 Model: "Person of Peace"

The Luke 10 model is powerful on several fronts. It requires little or no money. It is radical in that the church is planted by a person passing through town, leaving the "person of peace" or some other local in charge. In this way it runs counter to our entire system of professional pastors and missionaries. In Jesus' plan, the nimble church planter simply pulls up stakes and moves if the field isn't fertile. Whenever the field is ripe, the church planter (apostle) hangs around long enough to disciple the person of peace, leaving that person(s) to pastor the new congregation.

This paradigm fosters rapid multiplication. And it is easy to reproduce. People from these "simple churches" can turn a job transfer into an opportunity to plant the church in a new location or country. Until recently, churches like this were seldom found in North America. They were the purview of developing nations. They also look much like the record of Paul's travels in Acts 13–19.

The Acts 2 Model: Gatherings, Both Great and Small

The Acts 2 model is more intrinsic to many churches in the West. It assumes strong "lay" involvement—where did they get leaders for all those home meetings? It displays a natural movement into leadership—Stephen, Philip and the others became the "noncoms" (non-commissioned officers) of the Jerusalem church. Philip later took the gospel to other cultures. Just like the picture in Luke 10, this model embraces multiplication of leaders and churches.

As a side note, large churches that do not develop cells stunt the growth of potential pastors. Hence, they seldom reproduce themselves.

The problem with either model is that we tend to compartmentalize Scripture. We stop reading when the 70 return from their mission. Or we put our Bible away after finding the Lord adding daily to the number of the early Christians after Pentecost. We simply fail to recognize the underlying congregational multiplier implied in both situations.

I submit that you should read the Gospels and Acts as a continuum. I apologize if this sounds patronizing—I know that you wouldn't be holding this book in your hands if you didn't know the Bible as well as I do. But still, I think compartmentalized thinking blinds us to the missional strategy that materializes in Luke's two accounts. Luke 10 was a training mission. Acts 2 shows the results of the training; then beginning in Acts 10, the gospel began its steady march across the world. Philip, Peter and Paul *did* Luke 10 in Samaria, Caesarea and on into Europe.

Could we plant churches in the simple manner laid out in the Gospel of Luke but watch them grow into something resembling the large complex of people described in the early chapters of Acts?

What's a Body to Do?

What should happen in a church meeting? That depends on your culture. For some, church should look like a Broadway musical. For others it resembles a college lecture hall. Still other churches resemble a rock concert. Some have the feel of an overgrown coffee shop. All are probably valid. But I am most happy when a church feels a little like a situation room on an air base. The people are there to discover and strategize their current mission.

What did a church meeting look like when it was invented? What's the prototype? In Acts 2:41-47, we find eight distinct *functions* of the church: the apostles' teaching, fellowship, the Lord's supper, prayer, shared meals, miracles, praise, generous giving and evangelism.

We know that the church met both in homes and in a large public place. And, each of the listed functions would best lend itself to one or the other—a large group or small. Finally, evangelism must have been a pretty private affair given the tidal wave of persecution that soon overtook those earliest Christians. "So what?" you ask. Well, location and group dynamics are *form* issues. Any architect or military planner you know will tell you that form necessarily follows function.

We gain further insight on form and function through Paul's letter to Corinth. He writes, "What is the outcome then, brethren? When you assemble, each one has a psalm, has a teaching, has a revelation, has a tongue, has an interpretation. Let all things be done for edification" (1 Cor. 14:26, *NASB*).

Paul's purpose for the passage is to pull an overenthusiastic church into the kind of order where everything could edify. But in so doing, he also reveals something of the nature of a church meeting—it was interactive. Everybody played. If we intend to effectively multiply, we need to get everyone into the act.

For our church, this is a constant problem. We are addicted to the weekend "show." We know how to throw a party and we have a team of great preachers. And we do sport a host of highly interactive home groups, *but* they only involve about half our people. The other half are doomed to a spectator's role if we don't persist in pressing for interactivity. Mind you, this is not for the sake of interactivity itself, but in order to equip our people for ministry off the church campus—in the real world.

I'm not trying to write an instruction manual for interactivity on the weekend in a large church. I am encouraging you to raise the bar in New Testament terms. Current church culture rewards a spectator's environment and has proven capable of raising large crowds while the surrounding world disintegrates. These are big issues if you intend to create a movement that makes demons quake.

Think Again

We need to rethink everything about our churches in light of the Great Commission. Toward that goal, here are some questions to ask: Are we effectively discipling nations? Could a single congregation affect change on every continent? How can a small church reach the ends of the earth—directly? Are our mission and purpose in alignment with each other? Does our own stated mission actually line up with the Great Commission? Could our congregation turn a couple of scriptural models into the multiplication machine they once were? Do our events and meetings involve people ministering to each other? Do we equip every moment and at every level?

PART 4

OPPORTUNITY IS WHERE YOU MAKE IT

15

TENACITY

. . . .

FAITH IN AN AGE OF FEAR

We sometimes lack the confidence that the Church will really penetrate the gates of hell. And it will not—it cannot—unless we believe it can.

While Britain stood alone, three months before the United States would join her in the war, on October 29, 1941, Winston Churchill addressed the boys at his alma mater: "Never, never, in nothing great or small, large or petty, never give in except to convictions of honour and good sense. Never yield to force; never yield to the apparently overwhelming might of the enemy." He got it—if we never *give in* to despair, we will never *give up*. Victory is born of unyielding hope.

I recently visited Amsterdam. This beautiful city was once the crown jewel of Europe. At one time, the Dutch East Indies Company was the richest in the world, outfitting Amsterdam with a system of canals rivaling the grandeur of Venice. At that time, Amsterdam was also a city of spiritual wealth. Reformation Holland was so Christianized that there is still hardly a spot in the entire country where you will not see a church steeple if you stand and turn in a slow circle.

Life Is Hard Without God

Yet, today, most of those churches are empty. And the results of godlessness are becoming quite visible. Like the rest of post-World War II Europe, Holland shed most of its Christianity during the Nazi devastation. The war brutalized the faith of most Europeans into remission.

During the immediate postwar era, the Dutch people found comfort in the brave new world of secular science. But secularism and its twin sister, materialism, offer no bulwark against the pall of Islamic terror now shadowing the minds of most Europeans. These cornerstones of postmodern society are also no panacea for the increasingly pagan behaviors on display in Amsterdam—or any big city in the world.

Young people mark their bodies with tattoos and piercings. God is whatever anyone conjures in his or her own mind—as in, "The god I would worship would never condemn someone to hell . . ." Sex is ever more vulgar and sold even more cheaply. Drugs are a given. Homelessness is a badge of merit for some. Graffiti blossoms everywhere, as does deconstructionist art. Violence lurks under a neon glare and in every night shadow.

The good news is that the church is again growing in Holland. And not just in Holland—all over Europe, church planters are at work. Without stately buildings, these new churches meet in homes, public schools and even in pubs. The European church is tiny but alive and growing. On the Catholic side of the fence, Pope Benedict II is doing his part to remind Europe of its Christian past. The future looks a little brighter each day.

Like Amsterdam, our big cities are the caldrons of culture. What takes place in the metropolitan arena will soon be standard fare in every suburb and village. Today, more than anything else our cities are cooking up a menu of despair. What our world needs is a reason to hope. We need hope more than we need any other commodity.

The message of the kingdom of God is a word of hope. Never separated from miracles of power, the apostles brought hope to the dying culture of the ancient Greeks and Romans.

The gods of the Greeks and Romans had let them down. At best they were mere statues; at worst, frightful demons. Then there was that political invention, the man-god. These often died at the hand of palace intrigue. The greatest of them, Alexander, may have conquered, but he died of syphilis, a frail human. By the time of the apostles, the once ethical republic of the Romans had morphed into the maniacal rule of a string of tyrannical Caesars. Go read a book about the gladiatorial contests or about the overt sexuality of ancient Rome—you will find much in common with our postmodern world. Couple this with the ever-menacing threat of the barbarian hordes and you will see how well our world parallels theirs. The ancient world was much in need of hope when the gospel was first announced. The results were astounding. Hope paves the way for the kingdom of God.

The King *Is* Coming

I recently heard an old song that painted hope all over the landscape of my heart. It shouts, "The king is coming! The king is coming! I can hear the trumpet sounding and now his face I see."

Those words promise victory over any despair the world dishes up. Jesus is coming to bring peace to this frantic planet. Author J. R. R. Tolkien hinted at the Lord's coming victory. You sense deep truth in that moment when Aragorn wraps his fist around the sword Anduril in *The Lord of the Rings: The Return of the King*. In doing so, he *stepped into* his own calling. Victory was his as soon as he did.

Victory is ours as soon as we engage the call of our Master, Jesus Christ. Our liege Lord is the victor. Success on the spiritual battleground is assured, though you and I may still see it only through a darkly tinted window. Like frightened hobbits, we often gape at the enemy instead of fastening our gaze on our champion. In those moments, we surrender faith to fear, falling backwards, useless to our cause.

Faith is a choice. We observe data. We weigh possibilities. Then we choose the most promising path. It is not fantasy. It is a spiritual weapon. The Scriptures say that faith is born of God. It is a gift from Him. It also says, "And this is the victory that has overcome the world—our faith" (1 John 5:4, *NKJV*). Do you get it? Our faith equals our victory. The very choice to trust God in the face of overwhelming circumstances is victory. Not a promise of victory, but actual victory. It triggers light in the heavens and shudders in the darkness.

Does your faith need a booster shot? Think about the apostle Paul describing faith as a choice to stand against adversity. He put it this way: "Don't be intimidated by your enemies. This will be a sign to them that they are going to be destroyed, but that you are going to be saved, even by God himself" (Phil. 1:28). The statement takes on more meaning when you understand that Paul wrote it from a prison, awaiting word as to whether he would live or die for his faith. Our very choice to trust God is a weapon against our adversary. In trusting Christ, we intimidate the intimidator.

Our faith is in a Person, not a doctrinal position. If it were, we would be in serious trouble. We trust God to work in us through the same Holy Spirit through whom He raised Jesus from the dead (see Rom. 1:4). I thank God that we needn't understand the mechanics of prayer, because I never will. I do understand that Jesus told us, "Ask, and it will be given to you; seek, and you will find; knock, and it will be opened to you. For everyone who asks receives, and he who seeks finds, and to him who knocks it will be opened" (Matt. 7:7-8, *NKJV*). When you and I choose trust in Jesus over obstacles, we win.

The king *is* coming. He's coming to New Jerusalem one day soon, but sooner than that to a neighborhood near you.

Where Is This Leading?

Yes, the world is a mess. But the last battle is a long way off. Jesus is still on the throne. The demons still shiver. Hope abounds when you look for it.

It's an age-old tradition for a boxing manager to throw a towel into the ring to signal defeat for his fighter. This only happens when it becomes obvious that the manager's man is wilting under the blows of his opponent. The goal is to protect the fighter from irreversible damage.

It is easy to want to throw in the towel when it comes to life on planet Earth. We Christians have reduced our faith to a formula—a philosophy that works well only for the most disciplined. Paul's question to the Galatians is appropriate for us: "Have you lost your senses? After starting your Christian lives in the Spirit, why are you now trying to become perfect by your own human effort?" (Gal. 3:3).

Modern Christianity has morphed into a kind of humanism cloaked in Godspeak. It can too easily degrade into a kind of legalism that is wrapped in the language of forgiveness. We offer justification by faith and then press people into what we call an "overcoming lifestyle." Without an *experiential* component, this can only work for tough-minded people. Without the power of the Spirit, we are only Christian humanists.

Christian humanism miscasts us as defenders of the faith. Worse yet, sometimes we try to defend the Lord Himself. We forget the meaning of the word "savior." This reversal of roles eats at our faith and probably causes us to get in His way rather than join Him in achieving His goals.

God gives us a thumbnail shot of role reversal in Romans 12. Paul quotes God as saying something like, "Get out of My way. Revenge is My business and I can fight My own fight." Actually, the text says "give place unto wrath," and then continues, "Vengeance is mine; I will repay, saith the Lord" (Rom. 12:19, *KJV*). At the very least, Paul is telling us to make room for God to operate. You get the picture—God can fight His own battles. Our job is to "announce . . . that the Kingdom of Heaven is near. Heal the sick, raise the dead, cure those with leprosy, and cast out demons" (Matt. 10:7-8). If we play our part with faith, He will do His with victory.

Thinking that we need to protect God or protect the faith, *we* often choose to "throw in the towel." Hear a little bad news and we assume our side is losing the culture wars. We slouch into obsessing over whatever horror story our favorite website serves up each day. We wilt over negative input—be it news of terrorism, poor economic returns or the erosion of moral values around us. Negative thoughts elbow us toward despair, which nudges us off a cliff into a kind of "holy" defeatism. We might as well modify the old anthem to sing, "Onward, Christian soldiers, *drooping* off from war . . ."

We are too quick to cry, "Maranatha" ("come quickly, Lord Jesus"; see 1 Cor. 16:22). Unsure of the fight for the soul of the planet, we want off the bus at the next stop.

Our greatest need is to keep the faith. We *can* overcome the world. We *can* turn the tide. Yes, we are in a war. But it is a war that we will eventually win. Remember, the book of Revelation in the Bible is not the revelation of the anti-Christ. It is the revelation of *Jesus Christ*. He wins! We win with Him! The battle is His to win, and He knows it.

Penetrating Islam

The Church, fully alive, is the only thing that can turn the world right side up. Jesus said the powers of hell would not conquer it (see Matt. 16:18). Small victories are everywhere but on the TV news. Let me tell you a story that will bring a tiny sliver of hope to your heart. It holds the keys to the kingdom of heaven in its grasp. Stories like this abound. Multiply them by the million and they can open doors to entire cultures. But stories like this will only occur if we believe our God is still in the fight—if we refuse to throw in the towel.

My friend Teri gave birth to a very sick baby boy. She was fortunate enough to enroll her child in the testing of some marvelous medical procedures at Johns Hopkins Medical Center in Maryland. There she met a beautiful young woman from an Islamic country, holding a small girl who had lost half her brain to surgery. The woman immediately warmed to Teri. Teri is a delightful warrior in the faith, constantly praying for others while she holds out for complete wholeness in her son.

As they talked, this lady told Teri that she knew God was punishing her through the tragedy that had befallen her daughter. By this time, Teri had already told the lady of her own faith in God, a God who heals small children. Though bent under a load of guilt and fear, the young Islamic mother told Teri that she identified with her because "the Muslim god is the same as the Christian God." Teri was able to explain to her that they do not worship the same God—that Jehovah is a healer, that Jesus cancelled guilt and that we have reason to hope because God is alive. She left her new friend a little bewildered, thinking, *Could there be a God who treats people with mercy rather than anger?* A little change of perspective crept into her heart during that conversation.

Did that woman become a Christian that day? No. Teri says she is not a great evangelist and never pushed the conversation to its possible conclusion.

However, that short encounter demonstrates spiritual hunger in the Muslim community. These are people just like us. They hurt over their children. They mourn lost lands. They envy those who are richer than they. And deep in their hearts, they long for a God who will love them. Islam looks like an enemy. Individually, Muslims are often the warmest people you'll ever meet. The answer to the cultural wars is always the same: "There is a God who loves you and has great plans for your life."

One Man and a Hundred Churches

I have a friend named Paul who visited Pakistan on a business trip in late 2000. The result of this one man's simple obedience is the planting of nearly 100 churches and the conversion of hundreds of Muslims. In the teeming metropolis of Karachi, Paul met a Pakistani (who must go unnamed) who had introduced more than 120 people to Christ.

This man is armed with a master's degree in marketing but lost his job after being promoted to full partnership in the company. It was after the promotion that the senior partners discovered that he is a Christian. They pressed him to convert to Islam. When he would not, they fired him for "dishonoring" the existing firm.

While living in poverty, his greatest outlet for discipleship was an Internet café. Whenever he could scrape together enough money he would write a Bible study, emailing it to everyone on his list. My friend Paul thought he heard the voice of God when he met this man. The Lord told him to inform this young Pakistani, "You are an 'apostle,' not an evangelist. These are not *your* converts, they are *My* pastors." The man received the instruction with zeal. He planted a church that month. That church birthed 97 others in a little less than four years. My friend Paul stepped forward with a single act of prophetic obedience. Through it God birthed frenzied church growth and evangelism.

Many of these churches number in the hundreds. The mother church approaches 1,000 on special occasions. Threats and violence against these people abound but their gospel comes with healings, signs and wonders. This is the church victoriously knocking at the doors of hell. Being Pakistan, the movement has already experienced a couple of splinters, but you can even find victory in that if you see it as a movement begetting other movements.

I have another friend who traveled all the way to Bangladesh to visit a child he had supported through World Vision. The result of that trip is an orphanage housing 45 children that he supports out of his own pocket. This man is successful, but not what you would call wealthy. Yet he is making a difference in the world. All of his kids regularly hear the gospel.

I have a hundred other stories like these. All are about the Church in victory. It is important that we in the United States hear them.

We are the richest nation on earth. We have rapidly developing technology at our disposal. We have the financial means to kick-start and support entire movements in other countries. We are highly mobile. Many of us do business internationally. Most of us could go on a mission to another country. We could easily partner with someone in a foreign land. In short, we have the resources the world needs. Hope in our hearts moves us to use these resources for the kingdom of heaven. We need the courage to keep fighting and leave that towel in the corner and stay in the ring. We must "never, never give in . . ."

MISSION

· · · · · · · · · · · · · · · · · · · ·

REACHING PEOPLE
WHERE THEY ARE

On the day prior to the Normandy invasion, Dwight David Eisenhower, the Supreme Commander of Allied Expeditionary Force, wrote two single-paragraph press releases. He tucked them into his pocket, knowing that in 24 hours, one would be useful. The other became a footnote to history.

One press release simply announced that the invasion had occurred and that men were successfully landed in France. The other would announce its failure and Eisenhower's singular and personal responsibility for that failure.

These were the actions of a brave man. Following months of planning, he would launch his army of *citizen-soldiers* against a deeply entrenched, battle-hardened foe. And at launch time, he had a window of just a few hours of clear skies before a storm would erase all possibility of success. Eisenhower was a taker of calculated risks.

This chapter and the next are intended to underscore the unmet opportunities we often face in church multiplication. They will point up the need for risk takers as leaders if we intend to take back a culture. Both chapters draw from two books, one I wrote called *Friends: The Key to Evangelizing Generation X,* and another entitled *The Churching of America, 1776-2005:*

Winners and Losers in Our Religious Economy by Roger Finke and Rodney Stark. *Friends* is out of print but floating around the Internet. *The Churching of America* is a newer book and definitely worth reading.

Tactical Opportunities

Ike's grand goal was the "unconditional surrender" of Nazi Germany. His strategic goal was to march armies into the heart of Berlin while cutting off all possible escape for Nazi leaders. Tactically, his need was to place a lot of boots on the ground at the place where he felt the enemy was the weakest. For us that translates into putting churches into places where spiritual needs and interests are higher than in other places.

These areas of spiritual opportunity take many forms. Most largely suburban and middle-class evangelicals will think immediately of newly developed communities. Others will look at the pain evident on the streets of urban America. And the daily news reminds us that we are increasingly surrounded by first-generation immigrants from repressive countries. Each of these categories, and others like them, presents opportunities to those willing to take a little risk for the kingdom of God. You could think of this in terms of a business looking to expand into new markets. The markets are there. Are you willing to do whatever is necessary to penetrate them? Will you put boots on the ground where the opportunity calls for them?

In 1776, the Congregationalists, Episcopalians and Presbyterians had a lock on the spiritual life of the new nation. They held a market share of 55 percent. There were just 65 recorded Methodist congregations at the time. And the Baptists were a divided force with perhaps 200 churches. In 1850, just 74 years later, there were more than 13,000 Methodist churches, enrolling 2.6 million members—more than one-third of all American churchgoers. Congregationalists—the leaders in colonial times—had stagnated at a half-million members. The Baptists were not far behind the Methodists, with 2 million members. The big three colonial powerhouses in those years didn't fare much better than the American auto giants today. In just 74 years their market share shrank to just over 19 percent.[1]

So what happened? It appears that the Methodists and Baptists were better prepared to go where the opportunities led. They took their leaders from the ranks of their members. Most pastors were bi-vocational, if they received any salary from the church at all. Most important, they rose from the ranks of the very population they would evangelize. A Methodist or Baptist pastor was usually a farmer cast in the same mold as those he would address with homespun stories and a heartfelt, though less than professional, understanding of Scripture. In other words, he talked the language of those he served.

Churches were small. Fellowship was intimate. Testimonies to answered prayer and changed lives were a large part of these churches. Much of church culture came from those attempts at mass evangelism, the camp meetings or from the Methodist "Classes," a small-group discipleship network. Pastors and leaders began as lay leaders in their congregations.[2] The power underneath all this lay in the ready availability of enough men to accomplish the task.

This was Eisenhower's problem on the beaches at Normandy. He needed first to get enough men ashore to hold the beachhead, and then enough to overwhelm the enemy. The approach of both Methodists and Baptists in those first seven decades of American nationhood allowed them to put leaders wherever there were people. On the frontier and in the newly developed cities, wherever there were people there were outposts of those two movements.

Media philosopher Marshall McLuhan coined two phrases that remain with us today: "the global village" and "the medium is the message." We in truth live in a global village. Air travel, global commerce and the Internet have made the world a much smaller place—a place abounding with new relationships that can serve as trailheads into church multiplication. I try to look at every new relationship with eyes on expanding the footprint of Christ's church.

The second phrase about the co-mingling of medium and message is endemic to every sermon we preach, but we often miss some of the larger implications. We want each follower of Jesus to live in ways that their life becomes their message. But we often overlook the impact we could have if we rapidly "credentialed" some of those very life messages to positions of pastoral leadership. Much of the explosive growth of the Church on the American frontier can be linked to the rapid multiplication of church-planting pastors—without the benefit of formal education (More on that in the next chapter.)

Paul as a Risk Taker

First, let's look at Paul as a risk taker when it came to sponsoring leaders. During seminars, I often ask people to carefully observe and discuss Paul's methods in Acts 13-19, and the messy stuff in his letters to the churches. This simple exercise opens eyes and exposes our own apparently over-cautious approach to ministry. Paul rapidly multiplied churches. He did so by betting on people he couldn't have known all that well.

Quick bets were his specialty as he spent precious little time with his converts before moving on. Leaving town was usually necessitated by persecution. The longest recorded stay in any one place was two years in Ephesus, less than half the time it takes to get through a Bible college in America. In most cities, he remained under two weeks. Yet everywhere he went, he appointed elders and established churches. He chose people who spoke the common language because they were common people.

At Pisidian Antioch, Paul was rejected and left the synagogue to minister to Gentiles in Iconium. Immediately persecuted, he fled to Lystra where he was driven out of town and stoned. He moved on to Derbe, where many were saved. Paul got pounded in town after town but seldom left without measurable results. After recovering in Derbe, he "returned again to Lystra, Iconium and Antioch of Pisidia, where they strengthened the believers. They encouraged them to continue in the faith . . . Paul and Barnabas also appointed elders in every church and prayed for them with fasting, turning them over to the care of the Lord" (Acts 14:21-23).

The evidence at Philippi is much the same—public preaching, a night in jail and then appointing elders on the way out of town. In Thessalonica, "As was Paul's custom, he went to the synagogue service, and for three Sabbaths in a row he interpreted the Scriptures to the people. He was explaining and proving the prophecies about the sufferings of the Messiah and his rising from the dead . . . But the Jewish leaders were jealous . . . that very night the believers sent Paul and Silas to Berea" (Acts 17:2-3,5,10). Again, he spent very little time in town, yet elders were appointed and a church established.

Problems and Solutions

With so little time given to proving and improving leaders, it isn't any mystery that half of every one of Paul's letters is filled with instructions to leaders and corrections to doctrine as well as sinful behavior. I wonder what the Methodists and Baptists were dealing with in early America?

Because of Paul's method, he created problems. More than simply making converts, he made disciples and appointed them as leaders of fledgling churches. He supervised by mail, from a distance. Without adequate and *continued* supervision, he could not have succeeded. He would have only chalked up a lot of false starts. We can improvise supervision issues and solve problems as we go. But if we don't put boots on the ground, we won't win any wars.

[Paul and his peers had more confidence than us in the process of appointing elders, as they "prayed for them with fasting, turning them over to the care of the Lord, in whom they had come to trust" (Acts 14:23). Maybe it was because they saw their own success in light of God's grace at work. For them, education played backup to the Holy Spirit. In our generation, it plays first string.]

Timothy

Paul rarely had the time to put into leadership training, as he was bound to leave town or die. It interests me that on the first missionary trip, he came back around to those cities after the fireworks and quickly appointed elders to lead the churches. The text doesn't say it, but I believe he worked with the natural leaders who had survived and shown themselves capable in the months or weeks since he had last seen them.

In any case, his criteria for selection were much different from ours. He had little opportunity to observe these people, and even less time to train them. In most cases, they were babes in Christ; yet they were elders in the sense that they had been saved longer than others in their community.

I've heard it argued that they already knew the Scriptures due to their Jewish upbringing. This sounds nice, but these people were Gentile God-fearers who would not convert to Judaism because of its rigors. It is hard to believe they were that well educated before Paul came to town. If they were, why did he write all those letters to correct their theology?

Elders and Youngers

The apostles' tactics were flexible and based on trust in the power not only of the gospel but also of the Holy Spirit. I want to live like that. The Bible says to "lay hands suddenly on no man" (1 Tim 5:22, *KJV*). That is a relative expression. "Elder" is a relative term. In a new church, you can trust leadership to younger men more easily than in a more established situation because the man is an elder compared to the others. I've taken chances in a new situation that I would never consider later on, and those chances have paid off handsomely. I based my actions on trust. Those people are now vindicated as heroes of our movement. First, there was trust that the Lord would reveal the right people through supernatural as well as natural means. Paul chose Timothy on the recommendation of "the brothers at Lystra." Secondly, there was also the trust that God would work with these people much as he had with Paul and his peers.

Faith

Most of the time we have too many *qualifiers* worked into our programs of ministry. It is hard to imagine John saying, "Repent and go to 12 weeks of confirmation before you can be baptized for your sins." There is a healthy immediacy to the New Testament movers that we lack today. Ministry must be left in the hands of the Holy Spirit. While we run sanitary operations, He brings great victory out of apparent disorder. While we are unwilling to take risks, He demands faith.

Dwight Eisenhower made a risky decision during World War II. We need to remember that most of his army was made of fresh recruits. Many had literally trained with wooden mock-ups rather than real weapons. They were fresh off the farms and streets of an isolated nation. Yet not only did they conquer a larger, better-equipped and experienced army, but they also went on to win the hearts of a sorely divided continent.

Eisenhower, much like Paul or those early American church planters, made decisions that went against conventional wisdom. Their actions may have looked foolish, and certainly drew criticism. But in retrospect those decisions worked—in fact, retrospect is so powerful that it mostly causes us to recognize the risks they took when they did the things they did. Faith seems to be an ability to see in advance what others will recognize only in the rearview mirror. These heroes from our past succeeded at their task, and we will as well; the only requirement is a step of faith.

EDUCATION

· ·

LEARNING FROM
AMERICA'S PAST

The American church was born in renewal—the Puritans brought it with them from Europe. The church has continued to thrive because of several major spiritual awakenings throughout its history. But even a spiritual awakening dissipates over time unless new churches are planted to contain and nurture the new converts. As these young Christians grow they become salt in the earth and bring long-term change to the secular society around them.

You could say the first Great Awakening (1730-1755) was the genesis of the spiritual drive behind the American Revolution. The Second Great Awakening (1790-1840) and the Mid-century Frontier Revival (1850-1900) certainly contributed to the eventual demise of slavery and to the recognition later on of women's rights. In each case, church planting played a strong role in preserving the work of the Spirit until it saturated the culture with salt and light.

If we need new congregations during times of renewal, we need them more when secular influence and even atheism seem to dominate popular culture. New churches evangelize, assimilate and influence people far more quickly than established congregations.

Church Multiplication Models from Acts

The book of Acts offers six fairly distinct training/multiplication models.[1] Each is worth our attention.

The Original Cell Church Idea

The first mention of church activity in Acts (chapter 2) suggests house-to-house meetings following a large celebration, approximated in today's *cell church* teaching. House leaders would have followed up the large group teaching of the apostles in an informal setting. The preaching of the apostles and informal discussion among the disciples were the primary training, closely following the relationship of Jesus and the Twelve. If you look at Acts 2:41-47, you'll see a list of church functions and be able to draw a pretty clear distinction between large-group and small-group activities. The important thing to note is that their number swelled from 120 to more than 3,000 in a single day. They needed a lot of home leaders in a hurry.

Pragmatic Expansion

The second incidence of church planting is what I call *pragmatic expansion of the church*. In short, the saints ran for their lives. It was most practical to leave Jerusalem in a hurry after the death of Stephen the deacon. But everywhere they went they preached what they knew.

Here, as well, the primary training agency was the teaching of the apostles. Those who ran and preached remain unnamed. What is recorded is their effectiveness in Samaria, Phoenicia, Cyprus, Cyrene and Antioch. These people may or may not have been intentionally discipled; that is not the point. The fact is that they had been effectively discipled. They produced results. And once they had results, they had to act like pastors, however much or little they understood what that meant. As effective evangelists they became pastors by default.

There was a measure control, however. The apostles were available to bail them out if their knowledge and gifts fell short, as in the case of Philip in Samaria (see Acts 8:4-8), or in Antioch with the arrival of the more experienced Barnabas (see Acts 11:19-24).

Spontaneous Combustion

Spontaneous combustion describes the birth of the church in Ethiopia. The eunuch had some knowledge of the Old Testament but needed the correction and instruction of Philip to know the Lord (see Acts 8:26-40). Without further instruction, he took the gospel home and Christianized a culture. For nearly 2,000 years this nation hailed the gospel as its cornerstone. The Holy Spirit overruled the ignorance of the partially educated eunuch. He grew into an evangelist and probably exercised pastoral gifts or else the church could never have penetrated the culture with such success. Form follows function.

Rapid Itinerant Birthing

Rapid itinerant birthing of churches followed Paul and his teams. This seems to be the primary message the Spirit conveys through what we term "The Acts of the Apostles." They are mostly the acts of one apostle who approximated the ministry of Jesus and His disciples.

It is important to notice the word "and" as it follows the name "Paul" throughout Acts. It is always "Paul and . . ." He made disciples and he planted congregations. It is also interesting to note that while two-thirds of the chapters in Acts describe Saul/Paul, far fewer mention the names of the other apostles. Acts is a record of rapid itinerant disciplemaking and establishment of congregations with those disciples as leaders. Paul and his friends preached, discipled for a pitifully short time and then organized churches around hastily appointed leadership.

The preponderance of training came afterward, as is apparent through the writing of the epistles. This model suffered from confusion, gross sin and lack of sufficient time for leadership training. It made up for the bedlam with those training manuals (the epistles), extensive travel (return missionary journeys) and confrontation. Its strong suit included quick penetration of cultures, rapid-fire church planting and the enduring legacy of the written Scriptures.

Primary-location Discipleship

Primary-location daily discipleship (a Bible school) is mentioned just once in the New Testament, but with astounding effect. When Paul retreated to the school of Tyrannus with just a few disciples, he remained for two years. The result was that all who lived in Asia Minor heard the gospel (see Acts 19:8-10). This is the only thing approximating a seminary experience recorded in the New Testament. It proved very effective, raising up more than 200 congregations in the metropolitan area of Ephesus. As I've said before, we need our seminaries. But my cry is that we also need to embrace every option that is available to us.

Single-minded Mentoring

Finally, we see evidence of favoritism, or *single-minded mentoring,* when Paul selected Silas and Timothy over John Mark and Barnabas (see Acts 15:40-41; 16:1-5). Strong *relational* communication of truth, much like the relationship of Jesus to the Twelve, may seem exclusive as it rewards like-mindedness and productivity in the disciple. This method provides unity and careful preservation of values as the mentor hands them off only to a trusted protégé. The strongest of the newer movements around us have incorporated this model to one degree or another.

My experience shows that the most productivity comes through that outstanding young man or woman who shows enough promise to grow close to the primary disciple-maker. The relationship usually bears fruit for three or four generations. Think Peter, James and John here, or Timothy and Silas. Perhaps a better example would be "Barnabas and Saul." Paul became the dynamo he was with much assistance from Barnabas. Those disciples who are in the group but not the inner circle produce results, but often it stops after one generation of multiplication.

A Flexible Approach

God is flexible, and we should follow His example. Biblical models are varied. We should keep all of them in our toolkit. New Testament leaders spent little time struggling with the finer details of technique. Baseline wisdom at this point equals that of the Nike shoe commercials: Just do it!

Current church-planting attempts largely reflect only one tool, the *primary-location discipleship* we call seminary or, in many cases, Bible college. *Local churches* are routinely left out of the mix when leaders decide to strategically multiply churches. Yet, local churches have the spiritual gifts and the leadership base necessary to evangelize a culture. We need to stretch our tent when it comes to the New Testament arsenal. What would have happened during the invasion of Europe during World War II if we had restricted the officer corps to graduates of West Point or Annapolis? The number of professionally trained soldiers and sailors was dwarfed by the number of those officers recruited from the ranks of industry and soldiers taught how to march while still fresh off the farm.

Three Effective Alternatives

Seminary, as the threshold to pastoral ministry, is a recent innovation in the United States. Prior to the establishment of seminaries, there were three predominant training patterns in place for pastoral ministry. First, Congregational and Presbyterian churches used a system of apprenticeship following college. Second, Methodist in-service training coupled circuit-riding apprentice preachers and lay leaders in home meetings. The circuit rider, while being discipled by a more established pastor, showed up for one sermon a month. The lay leader was the actual shepherd and ran the rest of the meetings. Finally, Baptists in the South ran their tent-making ministries. This was used most effectively in the South and on the frontier.[2]

After the Methodists, the Baptists offered the least formal training. They often merely chose the most gifted man in the congregation. He was licensed and ordained with or without the support of the neighboring churches. The Baptists' system allowed for rapid proliferation of churches.[3] Because Christian influence was weak on the frontier, the Baptists were best positioned to make a difference. Their rapid-fire expansion overwhelmed the surrounding unstructured and violent society. Unburdened by the educational costs and time constraints of the other movements, they also enjoyed the advantage of a pastor who reflected the culture of his parishioners.[4] The less formal the educative process, the faster the growth. Baptists would recruit a man based on giftedness and desire. No attempt at formal training was required of a church planter or pastor away from the big cities.

We've already looked at the rapid expansion of Methodists and Baptists from the onset of the American Revolution until 1850. The century between 1850 and 1950 reveals better understanding of the relationship between multiplication of leaders and that of new congregations. The Southern Baptists far outstripped the others in the number of congregations, leaping to 77,000 churches by 1950, while the Methodists had slipped back to 5,800 churches—just about half the number they boasted in 1850.[5] And the Southern Baptist membership numbers are just as impressive as their growth of congregations, having gone from 100,000 members in the year 1800 to 20,000,000 by 1960.[6] The difference in "production numbers" can be traced to the Methodists' drift toward a highly inclusive pattern of professional training for clergy during that 100-year period. The Methodists founded their first seminary in 1847.[7]

It is important to note that Baptist churches, and particularly the Southern Baptists, have built some of the finest colleges and seminaries in this country. But they did not fall prey to limiting access to the ministry to those high-threshold operations. They still work with "lay pastors." While building scholastic institutions, they strictly protect the concept of the locally trained and lay-led mission church. In fact, many seminarians adopt and act out the Baptist mission model of church planting concurrent with their classroom experience. This is an idea that is gaining momentum with the onset of the house-church movement. It is not unusual to see seminarians of any stripe launch home-based congregations during their years of schooling. I think that is a refreshing and innovative blending of the tools the New Testament offers us.

Missionary Wisdom

Any system we adopt ought to reflect a certain universality. It should be supra-cultural and not just the product of our own local or national interests. My own denomination, the Foursquare Church, has long built upon the shoulders of locally trained pastors while building Bible schools adjacent to large founding churches. Overseas, they've used schools to generate *extension programs* for those trained in the trenches.

Missionaries use every means available to them in developing nations but we often question those very methods in a developed nation like the U. S. or Japan. In 1973, hailing its success in the missions field, my denomination opened the door for lay pastors in U. S. churches. This crack in the door became a floodgate. We grew by nearly 50 percent in 20 years. Today, nearly 60 percent of our pastors are people who entered professional ministry without a formal theological degree. Most continue to pursue education as an enhancer to ministry rather than as a gateway into service. Faithful and fruitful ministry in a local church is the new gateway into ministry for us.

A look across the Pacific Ocean provides more food for thought. Japan displays evidence of an inverse relationship of the value of higher education. The Japanese sustain the most highly educated and professionally paid clergy in the world while showing little in terms of results.[8] While Japanese national church growth (with a professionally trained clergy) has been among the slowest in the world, the country shows great success wherever lay-led movements work in equal partnership with professionally trained leadership. In days gone by, the only real revival this country ever had bore witness to the effectiveness of locally trained clergy and the ensuing spontaneous multiplication of churches.[9]

Opportunity Knocks

Imagine we were living five centuries ago. The agenda in Columbus's day *should* have been to forsake the Asian dream in order to take advantage of the rich opportunities of the Americas. Narrowness of thought formed such a barrier that it took another 200 years before Europeans saw the Americas as anything but an obstacle God had put in their way to block the sea lanes to Asia. We can turn opportunity into obstacles if we aren't careful.

We should remember that the New Testament church had a very low threshold into the ministry and presents a pattern that works well to this day. We tend to see the early Christians as crude and unlearned, so we overlook their strategies. We would do well to expand our thinking to include what they already discovered.

Here are five suggestions that could create a new paradigm for rapid expansion of the church.

Take a Lesson from the Methodists and Baptists

There is much for us to learn from the history of our Methodist and Baptist friends. Their historic model remains one of the most flexible and widely encompassing of any missional model ever attempted. From them we learn that we should strive to build the best institutions we can while protecting the pathway of informal training and spontaneous generation of ministry. We should not restrict the mentoring process with requirements beyond discipleship and the confidence of local elders. We should also offer more and better in-service training options to the pastors who have not had the benefit of formal schooling. But even then, leave these as *options*; do not construct a new and higher, though informal, threshold to ministry. If a man pastors without any more than the training of his mentor, do not disqualify him through an educational system.

Link In-service Training to Seminary

Local churches are the centerpieces of all ministry. They *are* the church. They are the natural mothers, and new churches grow most easily when born from within them. We should view our schools as providers of curriculum and leadership for in-service training. The schools could supply scaled-down curriculum and function as an accrediting agency for locally operated in-service training, perhaps in the form of what some call "ministries institutes." Videotaped classes via the Internet, coupled with a live discussion leader and proxy, could extend classroom boundaries. Some schools have experimented with "extension campuses" with mixed results. Whatever works, works. But we must be careful not to raise standards to the point of excluding a Spirit-gifted individual who lacks the opportunity schooling presents.

Expand Our Vision

Bob Buford wrote a wonderful book called *Half Time*. It challenges midlife, mid-career people to rethink the purpose for their lives. The book functions as a vision expander for church members living lives on hold. It ought to be a wakeup call for leadership. We sit on powerful resources in our churches. We have the ability to tap into a body of well-grounded Christian personnel looking for midlife career change and new challenges. Potential church planters are all around us.

Beyond this leadership pool, our churches are bursting with untapped moneys that could go to church multiplication. Grassroots financial support flows easily if the church planter is a close friend or previous partner in some ministry.

And we can help launch a new congregation by either giving away or "loaning" members to form the nucleus of a new church. We should anticipate congregations in closer proximity in order to fully saturate communities with our influence. Again, local churches can best call the shots because of their intimate knowledge of their own territory.

Target Inner City and Cross-cultural Opportunities

Many seasoned "laypeople" could start a house church in their own immigrant culture or inner city neighborhood. Our history shows that we can enlist them if we are willing to acknowledge the gifts and work of the Holy Spirit in their lives.

One man, and his wife, in our church pastors two congregations of young adults living in a gang-ridden neighborhood. He is more than twice the age of any of his leaders and has never been in a gang. He became friends with a couple of gang members and began inviting them to church. When his car could no longer handle the number of the kids, they started a small church in a garage. Many of the early comers were still involved in unsavory behavior. They've been meeting for several years now, having seen several young men attend adult school to gain a high school diploma. Weddings have been performed and friends brought to Christ. The current situation is that this man pastors a second congregation with his leading disciple pastoring the original group, with the founder's wife staying on as a coach. The church is both inner city and cross-cultural (to our congregation and to its founder).

Anticipate Some Breakage

There will be some failures involving lay-trained pastors, and they will be held up as examples of proof of the need for formal training. However, for every example of an informally trained failure, you would not need to search very hard to find a *parallel example* of failure among our formally trained brethren. Problems happen. That's why Paul wrote all those exhortations and instructions in the epistles. The best advice here is, "Get over it!" We need to get on with the harvest and be willing to pick up a few pieces along the way.

A Challenge

We must challenge, even dare, our churches to reproduce pastors and stop depending upon seminaries and colleges to do the whole job. People give birth to their own children. It would be foolish to ask the hospitals to stand in as surrogate parents.

I am not trying to blow up seminaries or Bible colleges. I am saying that we had better add something to the current equation if we want to evangelize an ever more distant generation. I am challenging all readers of this book to get their hands dirty and take on the gospel. A spiritual awakening is born in repentance and moves on through evangelism. In order for it to awaken a culture, it must result in church planting.

18

A SECOND LOOK

· ·

EMERGING URBAN
OPPORTUNITIES

When we think of urban America, many people envision violent scenes on the evening news. Most middle-class Christians
immediately switch to other images . . . and other priorities.

Turning off to the urban scene overlooks two powerful opportunities for the church. The first is that of partnering with
churches and leaders living in our most difficult neighborhoods. The second has to do with the tidal shift that is gentri-
fication of the inner city, with the poor moving to the suburbs.
I want to briefly address both subjects.

Partnering with the Urban Poor

My friend Rod Koop looks after church multiplication efforts
in my denomination. Rod will tell you in a minute that he's
never planted a church. In fact, his business card carries this
statement: "I bring nothing to the table." So, you ask, "What's
a guy like that doing overseeing church multiplication efforts?" The answer: "Wonders." Rod is a natural networker. He
pulls people together with resources and like-minded others.
The results are phenomenal.

Rod's statement about bringing nothing to the table
compares with Dwight "Ike" Eisenhower's military career

prior to being given oversight of the entire European war. Ike served as a Major in the United States Army until 1940, when he made the rank of Colonel. He had never seen battle, having spent much of his career as a military planner, a role that did two things in preparation for the huge task he inherited. First, it kept him outside the inner circle of general officers—he was never party to the "correct" way of doing things. Second, he was forced to critique the decisions those Generals had made in the past. His seemingly insignificant role set him up as a unique strategic thinker when the big job came along. You might say he brought "nothing to the table" when he became Supreme Commander of Allied Forces in the European effort.

One of Rod Koop's greatest successes is with the African-American community stretched across the eastern and southern states of our country. He's tapped into an organic network of young men with vision. Some are from our movement, but many operate independently. Most had more vision than financial resources. Rod funds some startup ministries among them. More important, he funds opportunities for them to get together and stoke each other's fire. The result is a wave of new churches in some pretty difficult neighborhoods.

Among Rod's friends are people who were, in a past life, recruiters for the large gangs organizing large networks across state lines. Remarkably, the gang recruiters operate much like the apostle Paul did 21 centuries ago. They travel to a distant city and hang out at basketball courts looking for kids who are natural leaders. They befriend their potential disciples, offering them the chance of a better life (in this case, more guns and money). You can imagine the effectiveness such a person has when he shows up offering a better life in the power of the Holy Spirit.

Churches are being planted and neighborhoods are slowly being changed. The work would be much quicker if we could establish better partnerships between large, financially powerful churches and the urban poor. This is and is not a racial issue. It *is* because poor people in America are often people of color. It *is not solely* a racial issue because many of the churches that could offer help if they could get connected are also people of color. The problem is that poverty divides people into classes and into different neighborhoods. We need more people like Rod Koop in our collective arsenal.

But even the idea of the "urban poor" is growing obsolete in some places. High fuel costs and long drive times conspire to gentrify urban neighborhoods while pushing the poorer people out to the suburbs with their longer commute. We need to be strategically aware of the re-urbanization of many of our big cities and its implications for church multiplication. If we don't, a couple of decades from now, the cities will emerge as spiritual deserts without a visible presence of the church. At the same time, new needs and opportunities will arise in communities that become home to the increasingly dislocated poor. You can lament these needs or look for opportunities among them. The glass is half-something—you decide if that something is *full* or *empty*.

A Different Urban Opportunity

My wife and I recently enjoyed one of the best vacations of our lives—in an inner city neighborhood in Southern California. Let me describe it to you. We stayed one block from San Diego Bay. At sunset each day, we leisurely strolled to the water to watch hundreds of sailboats scurry back and forth across the calm surface. To do so, we crossed two major boulevards delivering thousands of people home from their day at the office or factory.

Looking around, we counted nine huge building cranes. They were erecting huge buildings that will house a combination of businesses and upscale residential developments. Just gazing up the hills behind our hotel, we could see another dozen or so condo projects in rapid development. San Diego's Gas Lamp District is actually its old "downtown." That is where the building cranes stood.

This kind of change is coming to the cities of America, and it won't stop because of a severe downturn in the economy. As world economies rise, the inner city building will ensue once again. High energy costs and rapid transit ensure the future of urban redevelopment. Buildings that went for next-to-nothing a few years ago are now among the most expensive real estate in our country. Flight to the suburbs has reversed itself. Urban living is now enviable. Wonderful restaurants and outdoor cafés abound. The parks are well manicured. The nearby combination of old industrial buildings and new recreational opportunities add to the joy of living in the again-flourishing business district.

Please forgive me if this is beginning to sound like an excerpt from an Orbitz advertisement. I am trying to describe the future of the Church. Most Americans share similarities with San Diego. Boston rebuilt its Back Bay neighborhood decades ago. New York has always been an urban playground with extremely high rents. Sacramento, Jacksonville and Dallas are in varying stages of residential development around the urban core. Even Honolulu has rebuilt Kakaako, an old industrial area adjacent to downtown, which already sports several mixed-use residential and office buildings.

The action isn't limited to the big cities. I recently visited Roseville, California, where the urban dream is being reignited in a small town, as it is in tiny Camas, Washington, and across the Columbia River in smallish Gresham, Oregon. City fathers everywhere are redeveloping their urban circles with a success only dreamed of when a few brave municipalities experimented with the concept in the 1970s.

Opportunity Knocks

Re-urbanization reeks with opportunity for the church. What greater break could you ask for? Thousands of people are now living in close proximity, actually meeting their neighbors in local pubs, at the grocery store and in the drycleaners. Millions more will soon follow. People in urban neighborhoods actually do interact in ways unheard of in the land of garage door closers and 15-minute drives to the shopping center.

Face-to-face contact, the one thing missing from suburbia, is rampant in an urban setting. When people really get to know each other, faith, or the lack of it, becomes more obvious. The neighbors will know who has the peace of God in their lives. Evangelism can, and will, occur more organically in this new situation.

But the successes of the urban planners also create major problems for church planners and leaders. We have gathered our forces around a suburban model ever since we got left behind in the 1950s. In those days, our problem was the support of huge "city churches" that had little parking to support the cars driven by the members who had newly moved to the fast-building suburbs. It took awhile for church planners to recognize that wave of migration to the suburbs. Once they did, they modified strategies with great success.

Later, as the suburban dream turned to something of a nightmare, city planners moved toward "ex-urban development," which is really a fancy term used to describe suburbs built *beyond* the suburbs. Those ex-urban neighborhoods boasted larger houses and wealthier people. They also became the target for church planters with great dreams. You could buy lots of land at country prices then wait for the population to arrive. The formula allowed for the easy development of many churches numbering members in the thousands. As the old suburban neighborhoods went into decline, land and buildings became increasingly available to church planners there. Decrepit shopping centers, bowling alleys and movie theaters allowed for the development of large churches.

The problem presented by urban development is its very success. High-density neighborhoods automatically present higher land costs. Because the neighborhoods are often more than a century old, subdivision occurred long ago resulting in tiny lot sizes. Add in the problem of zoning, which churches have faced over the years, and we are going to have to do some creative thinking. Here are some questions to answer if we are to re-salt urban neighborhoods with the gospel:

- Will we be zoned out because these are residential neighborhoods requiring ungainly setbacks from streets and neighbors?
- Will church properties be taxed (an idea that has a certain amount of momentum in Hawaii, because churches occupy land that could generate income for the state)?
- Where will we get enough land to build on?
- Should we adopt new models and abandon the idea of the megachurch?
- If churches must be smaller due to limited real estate, how will they afford to pay their pastors?

The questions I have outlined are real. The list is also not exhaustive. There are probably dozens more issues. The point here is simply that we must begin to think differently than we have if we are to meet this challenge.

Innovation is born of an admixture of adversity and faith that something good can emerge from a difficult situation. "Now faith is the substance of things hoped for, the evidence of things not seen" (Heb. 11:1, *KJV*). We haven't *seen* what God can do in an urban setting since the days of Aimee Semple McPherson or W. A. Criswell. But that is no excuse for not anticipating the opportunities that are coming our way. As we face our urban future, we should be mindful of two lessons from Scripture: (1) "No eye has seen, no ear has heard, and no mind has imagined what God has prepared for those who love him" (1 Cor. 2:9); and (2) "But my God shall supply all your need according to his riches in glory by Christ Jesus" (Phil. 4:19, *KJV*).

If we are willing to do some serious thinking, we will begin to know how to pray. God will supply, and we may actually experience a reawakening to the gospel. The harvest is truly plentiful. As America rediscovers its urban landscape, the church must run to keep up with the action. Every household that moves into the newly developing inner city represents another opportunity for the gospel. But there are obstacles we must deal with.

Density Punishes While It Blesses

Because redeveloping urban neighborhoods are so dense, they provide great opportunities for evangelism and Christian service. Neighborhood fairs and sporting events abound with the likelihood of gaining name recognition for newly formed congregations. You can give away free sodas, hand out literature at booths or participate as T-shirt-adorned volunteers.

People living in close proximity get to know each other in ways that simply don't happen in suburban areas. The chance meeting in a Borders or Barnes and Noble bookstore will lead to the question, "What are you reading?" That question can be a great way for someone to crack the door open, displaying a little of his or her faith. Neighborhood coffee shops seem designed to offer networking solutions to personal problems as new friendships grow from old ones.

However, increased population density can punish the church even as it creates opportunities for growth. Expensive land and small properties banish the idea of business as usual for Christians who have grown up thinking in suburban terms. A stand-alone church building with an oversupply of parking is a myth in the newly redeveloped inner city. Zoning problems will follow any attempt to construct large church buildings that take property off the tax rolls of cities struggling to keep up with urban development. So what's the solution?

Thinking Differently

We need to think in new paradigms if we are to overcome the land issues. A brief look at Japan could give us some quick insights to solving the space dilemmas we will face over the next three decades. Tokyo, once the most expensive city on earth, also boasts incredible population density. This makes it a dream for future-leaning thinkers.

In Japan, more people use public transportation than drive cars. Shinjuku Station hosts 440,000 train riders each day. Crime is virtually nonexistent due to tough laws and policing. McDonald's sells hamburgers from three-story restaurants. Even hardware stores have long since gone vertical, with the largest chain operating stores with two floors of office and nine for shopping, including three floors underground. Some "shopping centers" locate in narrow buildings seven or eight stories tall. And churches operate in rented office space or in stand-alone structures three or four stories tall. Many incorporate an apartment for the pastor in the upper story.

Since the end of World War II, the churches, which prospered in Japan, are those that have been able to change with the times. "New wineskin" churches, led by people "wary as snakes and harmless as doves" (Matt. 10:16), learned to exploit the urban environment for the gospel.

Japan isn't alone in its reach for the skies. Big cities around the globe experience these phenomena. You'll find similar examples in Chicago, San Francisco or New York. But Tokyo is probably the global test tube for vertical development. It may also serve as a roadmap into our future.

What's It Going to Take?

Several scenarios present themselves as plausible options for the re-urbanizing future. It is doubtful that any single strategy will dominate as a one-size-fits-all tool for ministering to the downtown crowd. And some of the ideas I offer will undoubtedly morph with others in the form of a model I haven't considered. But here are a few ideas.

The Charismatic Miracle Worker

This is the guy who will prove me wrong about all my assumptions in this chapter. There will always be a few gifted people who can drive any model, anywhere. Someone will find a way to build a megachurch on a huge piece of property in a downtown environment. And I say more power to them. The problem with this person as a model for others is that he or she has unique gifts that are hard to duplicate. Or there is the possibility that such a person achieves success by finding that *one piece* of cheap land that allows for the suburban past in the urban present. Don't bank on enough of these folks to solve the problem of evangelizing the reemerging downtown landscape. But do embrace them when they come along. They are a benefit to everyone.

Old Congregations Revived

Putting new wine in old wineskins is a tough call. But it can and will be done. Possessing a building solves difficult issues such as zoning and big mortgages. The problem here is the congregation. Fitting younger and hipper new residents to the older and often suburban commuters who often populate remaining urban churches will require a kind of miracle worker as pastor. It will most likely be done in those congregations that own a building but have lost all but a handful of members.

Public Schools or Meeting Halls

Equal access legislation will allow some churches to plant in public schools and other municipal facilities. These represent lots of space, cheap rent and an easily identifiable location. Having pastored for nearly 15 years in a public school, I highly recommend this option. The downside comes from a lack of enough such properties to house all the churches we need to plant. As salt in the earth, we need to think in terms of saturating a city with the gospel.

Rundown Urban Properties

Redeveloping downtowns are a crazy quilt of development. The housing core usually emerges in an area that was recently home to loft apartments in rundown brick buildings that once served as office or manufacturing centers a century ago. A few blocks away, glass and steel giants host the current financial center of the community. A couple of blocks in another direction all but the choicest older buildings are falling under the wrecker's ball. Their immediate destiny is reincarnation as parking lots. Look another direction and you will find industrial properties dating back to prewar America. Most remain in use, but many sit vacant as prospective tenants opt for newer industrial parks with better access to transportation services. These buildings present the perfect opportunity for a visionary church planter. The difficulties accompanying them are the ugliness of the neighborhood and the fact that they can be dangerous areas after dark.

Apartment-sized Congregations

The house church idea may be an answer to the saturation question. Someone with a vision for planting hundreds of "churches" numbering fewer than 20 people each would find an unlimited supply of meeting space available. The problem here would be that of paying the pastor. Twenty people can't afford a full-time, seminary-trained leader. But, a model that cast a traditional pastor as more of a planter/overseer (dare I use the word "apostle"?) could provide a solution.

Borrowing from the apostle Paul, a leader might start new meetings wherever he or she found interested people. After a few weeks or months, leadership of the fledgling congregation could be handed off to an emerging natural leader. The founder could continue to disciple that leader in an ongoing relationship. If an individual congregation suddenly found itself with rapidly accelerating growth, the group could look to rent office space or one of the other options I've outlined.

However you shake it, redeveloped urban areas are in our future. We need to strategize how to exploit the opportunities they present while solving the difficulties that will inevitably arise. You may be sitting in the midst of just such opportunities without having recognized them. Opportunities come mostly in the form of relationships with clusters of people living or moving into areas where a church could be born. It becomes our privilege to network those we know with others and with the knowledge that can empower them to become a new church.

PART 5

YOU *CAN* DO THIS!

19

FUN

· ·

CHURCH MULTIPLICATION
IS LIKE MAKING BABIES

God gave us sex. And only the worst kind of prude would ignore the fact that sex is equal parts fun and reproduction. It is
as *fun* as it is *effective* in filling the earth.

Babies come naturally to healthy families. They are the
product of human love and intimacy. Such love and intimacy
naturally result in the multiplication of the human beings that
enjoy it. Likewise, church multiplication isn't just a mechani-
cal process, but the result of healthy love and disciplemaking.
It ought to be fun.

Overcoming Sterility

Every so often I find our church growing sterile. I awake to realize that we have no one on deck to plant another church.
So what do I do? I pray. I ask the Lord of the harvest to raise
up labor for His harvest. Then I wait. I wait until someone says
something that sounds like the voice of the Spirit matching
his or her vision with mine.

It may be a casual comment about vocational ministry.
I may see pastoral potential in a person who keeps bringing
new people into faith. Or there are those people who never
travel alone because they shepherd naturally. However it

shakes out, I then sort of spy out that person. I want to see what God is putting into that person's heart without their knowing what I am doing—the last thing I want is for someone to follow "Ralph's calling into ministry." This must be a work of the Holy Spirit.

After weeks or months of observation, I openly challenge the person to take the next step into deeper relationships with the people around them. This nearly always takes the form of launching a MiniChurch, our form of small group. I also network them into new relationships within our discipling system. This is all informal. We run no schools.

If the person steps up to more intense discipling relationships, both as teacher and learner, I assume that we are pregnant. After a gestation period, we will launch another church. No nine months here, either. We don't specify how long it takes to ready a new church or a church planter. We usually want to see a string of three MiniChurches before we believe a person could truly plant a church. On the other hand, the process has occasionally been as short as a few months if the potential planter was already leading something that looked a lot like a church but didn't see itself as one. And we usually put several years into the relationship before moving across the ocean.

My point here is that new churches are best born of love and relationships. The "moment" of pregnancy happens when the minds of two or more individuals come together with a common vision. It's a pretty simple process. And, while some church planting models could be likened to unhealthy sex or a one-night stand, a healthy church plant is born of long-standing friendships. This is why we don't do short-term intensive training for potential church planters. For us the longer-term relationship gives a far better prediction of success than would be possible with any short-term training. The church is a relationship best built upon enduring rapport.

Finally, the new church must bear the DNA of the parents, and it will need their nurture. Church planters who receive strong, ongoing coaching succeed. Those left to their own devices usually struggle or fail.

The Law of Trees and Fruit

The Bible teaches that we can know a tree by its fruit. The actual context points to the moral fiber of a fellow human (see Matt. 7:16-18), but the parable is drawn from the fact that the natural fruit of a tree is tied to the DNA of the tree that gave it life.

This brings us to a question about the true fruit of a tree. Is the fruit of a coconut tree that creamy, sweet-tasting fiber that we eat? Is it the cluster of coconuts crowding the branches swaying in the wind? Is it another coconut tree? I say the true fruit of a coconut tree is none of the above. The true fruit of a coconut tree is actually a *coconut grove*. The tree is ultimately trying to reproduce itself *many times over*. It only produces coconuts as a means to a greater end.

Here in Hawaii, we are surrounded by coconut trees. We like to think of our church as a coconut tree that drops off coconuts that soon take root, growing into new trees that repeat the process. Some of our church multiplication efforts resemble coconuts that float across water for great distances before finding soil in which to put down their roots. Our church plants may cross vast oceans, but they eventually grow into mature trees that reproduce themselves again and again.

Strangely enough (or not so strangely when you think about it), I received a prophecy about my ministry becoming like a coconut tree long before I had ever seen one. While pastoring in California, my wife, Ruby, and I attended a convention in the snowy mountains of Colorado. It was there that Jack Hayford pulled us together and told us that God was going to make our ministry "like that of a tall palm tree, planted high above a city, that would give off coconuts that would sprout into many other trees."

The prophecy, suggestion, or whatever you choose to call it, occurred just after we had launched our first daughter church. God certainly brought Jack's words to pass. But for that to happen, we had to intentionally focus on the idea that it is as natural for a church to reproduce churches as it is for its members to reproduce converts. We had to *choose* to multiply our church or it never would have happened.

The Laws of Reproduction Are Natural

We reproduce in kind. Usually, people think of this in terms of ethnic heritage. But I think it goes farther. Bible study leaders create apprentices in their likeness. Youth workers do the same. This is the way we expand the "reach" of the ministries in our churches. We understand reproduction quite well *until* it comes to our pastors. We seem to forget that the laws of reproduction can apply to pastors as well.

A pastor who has it in his job description to reproduce himself will find it quite simple to turn out men and women with vision for church multiplication. Such a pastor will reproduce himself many times over.

By the way, did I mention that professors tend to reproduce professors—not pastors? This law of reproduction is what makes it tough for young seminary graduates to communicate in practical terms with church members rather than *struggle* to fill the hearts of quite ordinary people with heavy theological truths. That's not to say that seminarians can't launch church multiplication movements, but it's a tougher call.

Reproduction and Maturity

Nature fairly screams that reproduction is a sign of maturity. You speak of a tree as mature only when it begins to launch seed-bearing fruit. The same goes for monkeys or even gnats. The ability to reproduce *is* the recognized sign of maturity. Wouldn't it be wonderful if we applied the same idea to pastors and churches? This would require a huge shift in thinking away from our programmatic approach to ministry.

We would place a higher value on time spent together, with a more mature leader pouring his or her life into a younger person. Exponential growth lurks in the concept that a church would view reproduction as the primary signifier of maturity. We would empower our pastors by calling them to reproduce their own spiritual lives and knowledge in the hearts of several young disciples. I'm talking about primary responsibility—right up there with preparing world-class sermons. Who knows, we might win our world to Jesus!

Only reproduction at a pastoral level will ensure the future of the church. The earliest Christians operated this way and were unstoppable in their invasion of the pagan world. We have replaced simple discipleship tools with much more sophisticated systems. Yet, we don't enjoy the success of the earliest Christians or of our brothers and sisters in some of today's poorest nations.

I once spoke with a pastor from one of the largest and most successful evangelical churches in America. He lamented that though they had sponsored a few people that he termed "hired guns out of seminary" to launch churches, they had never "organically" planted a church under the leadership of someone raised from salvation and nurtured into pastoral ministry within their own congregation. He determined to change that. His cry could be a wake-up call for us all.

The job of multiplying ministry is best done by those who are in the ministry. Our problem isn't one of resources, but of a paradigm that needs rethinking.

20

HARDWARE

· ·

COLORING OUTSIDE
THE LINES

When my grandchildren were small, they scribbled outside the lines in their coloring books. My wife would patiently help them develop the skill to color inside the lines. A couple of years later she encourages them to draw outside the lines—actually on blank paper. They've learned to draw and they do it quite well. They've graduated from coloring books to art.

The thought of coloring outside the lines brings me to a question: What do you *do* when someone asks, "I just became a Christian; should I quit my sleazy job?"

Oddly Positioned Converts

I occasionally encourage people who are "oddly positioned" at the time of salvation to stay in that spot as long as the Spirit allows in order to penetrate the darkness around them. This occasionally results in the birth of an unconventional church.

Liquor Store Evangelism

Years ago, I met a new follower of Jesus. He worked in a liquor store across the street from our church in Hermosa Beach, California. We encouraged him to keep his job after getting saved. He wasn't so sure if it was the right thing to do. But he trusted me and stayed there. And he brought more than 30 people to the Lord in just over six months. He finally quit that job for one that paid better in another industry. He is now the outreach pastor in a large church he helped to start in Maui.

Prostitutes and Addicts

Recently, a young woman accepted the Lord and began wondering if she should quit her job. She was paid to hand out condoms and needles on some pretty mean Honolulu streets, in the middle of the night. I understand that her job skirts the issues of freedom from drugs and Satan's destruction of human life. The real question was whether she could leverage her relationships into ministry opportunities. The great thing is that this girl's unbelieving (and antagonistic toward traditional churches) bosses allowed her to bring her newfound Jesus into the lives of those she served.

This is a very brave young woman. She's totally fearless about sharing her faith. She has many friends among her "clients" who would never listen to me. Some are gay; others are drug addicts; still others are prostitutes. They need to know that God loves them.

Because she is on the streets every night, she has been able to lead several people to the Lord—people you wouldn't find in church. One of those men she led to Christ renounced homosexuality and was on the way to a heterosexual marriage when he died of AIDS due to his old lifestyle. One of our pastors conducted his funeral and preached a clear gospel message to more than 200 really hurting people. Several made a profession of faith in Christ at that funeral.

This young woman recently started a daytime Bible study, in a park, with three prostitutes. It is actually a simple church—the only one they will know until they move out of the park and off the streets. So we now have a small "pocket" church with a woman pastor operating in a red-light district in Honolulu.

A church like that fits almost no one's paradigm except that of an ex-junkie who found the Lord and moved out of the same park. He upbraided me for bringing food and clothes to homeless people on Christmas day. His advice: "If you want to do something *real*, come play softball with these people every Sunday, then hold a church service for them. Don't expect them to come to your suburban church. Start one for them where they live. Then you will be doing something that can last. Stop with the 'hit-and-run Christianity.' " Those are wise words from a wise man. I am ashamed to write that we did plant that church, only to see it fail after about a year. We had failed to multiply leaders, and the pastor moved off island without providing a replacement.

We know of no one else trying to bring salvation to these broken people. In a perfect world, we could raise enough money to hire the young woman who ministers in a red-light district as a missionary to that neighborhood. Until then, we get to keep her there with the world paying for it.

Please understand that this isn't a reckless stunt to encourage a new Christian to remain in a place most church members wouldn't go. It is not even normal practice for us. Most of the time, I encourage people to get out immediately. But occasionally, I meet a Christian who seems anointed as an evangelist, or someone who shows unusual leadership skill with difficult people. I encourage those few to remain as underground missionaries until the Lord urges them to leave or until they are pressed to leave by their employers. I would tell a DJ on a radio station that played a lot of trashy music to stay and bring salt and light into his situation. And before you go legalistic on me, we never encourage prostitutes, topless dancers or drug dealers to keep their jobs. However, I have seen a couple of bartenders bring people to the Lord before getting fired for doing so.

We Need to Shed "Propriety"

My take on all this comes from past experience. I began pastoring at a time when revival was in full swing. Much of the impetus for that movement came from dramatic conversions on the sleazy streets of Hollywood and the drug-ridden beach towns of Southern California.

As a fresh-faced graduate of a pastor factory, in a three-piece suit, I didn't fit well with my own congregation. I had to shed "propriety" in order to succeed. I would either change or lose the congregation the Lord was building around me. I wasn't enamored with the prospects of becoming a used-car salesman, so I decided to change. The Holy Spirit did much that ran against the grain of everything I had learned in church or school. But His deeds did fit with what I read in Acts.

Multiplying Unorthodox Churches

Our first daughter church looked like an accident. A group of hippies came into our church dragging along their leader (who didn't trust me at all). Eventually, this guy, Richard, and I became friends. We began walking the perimeter of a golf course in Palos Verdes, California, every Monday morning, just talking about the Lord and about ministry. We slowly built trust and a solid friendship.

At that time, we discovered the history of Dawson Trotman, founder of the Navigators. It was important to us that we were walking the same hill that he had walked 30 years before. We began to wonder if God was trying to teach us some of the same lessons about multiplying disciples that He had taught Trotman and his friends.

At that time, some of our members expressed concern that it was hard for them to bring their young children to church on Sunday evenings (church tradition in those days dictated attendance on Sunday morning, Sunday evening and Wednesday nights). Our answer was to send Richard to hold "Sunday night service" in one of their homes. After a couple of months, they decided they wanted to become a separate congregation.

Of course, I told them this was impossible because Richard hadn't been to seminary or Bible school. However, to contextualize all this, he was leading five rapidly growing Bible studies each week besides running his own business. Eventually, the Navigators picked up on his talents and recruited him to move to New Zealand as a missionary. That woke us up. Crossing cultures was easier than starting a church, and we decided to get with the program and launch the church.

Our denomination had no policy for "untrained" pastors. So we decided it would be easier to get forgiveness than permission—and it was. When I "apologized" for breaking three of their rules with what was an unheard of thing, "a church planting a church," they simply embraced the new congregation with love and grace.

The new church decided not to join the denomination, and even that decision was met with love and grace. For us, the horse was out of the barn. The troops were on the beach. We had multiplied the church.

You ask, "Did everyone offer love and grace?" Absolutely not. Local pastors criticized us heavily. Once, someone challenged Richard as to his training and adequacy for ministry. His reply, "Well, Jesus was a carpenter, and so am I. Besides that, I was discipled by Ralph Moore." I was embarrassed when

I heard it, but he was right on both counts. The Bible teaches us to train leaders through discipleship—carpenters, fishermen, etc. We are discovering that the call goes further to land developers, doctors and marketing consultants.

An effective invasion of this world demands that we break our traditional paradigm for church. Here are a few more radical examples.

The Gynecologist

When I pastored in California, Tom, the man who preached in my absence, was a young medical doctor who also taught at UCLA. Our church council's succession plan was that he would step into my role, at least temporarily, if I ever went down in a plane crash.

Tom eventually moved to Northern California and I moved to Hawaii. A seminary-trained pharmacist succeeded me in that church (it was where he first met Jesus). Tom began teaching an adult Sunday School class at a large church in his new hometown. Discovering doctrinal differences with that congregation, he met with the pastor to offer his resignation. That wise man suggested that instead of simply resigning he should take whoever would follow him and launch a new church.

This became a cross-denominational church plant with a pastor who had no formal training for ministry. The church grew to a size that forced Tom to choose between careers. He passed the baton to his associate. The church is large, owns property and has multiplied several times. And Tom is still the supply preacher when the pastor travels.

Church in a Bar

Six years ago, David, a new convert, was part owner and bartender in a pretty notorious Honolulu nightclub. Through our church, he was set free from alcohol and cocaine addiction. He grew close to one of our leaders who was bristling with vision to plant a church in that part of town. Unable to find meeting space, David got his partners to loan us the facility for a church plant on Sunday mornings.

Several positive things ran behind that decision: (1) We were able to start a church when no one else would rent to us; (2) many of the patrons of the club visited the church and became followers of Christ; and (3) perhaps the best result is that David is a copastor in the church he helped start.

The congregation eventually left the bar for larger quarters. They took several *former* bar patrons with them. Also, at least one marriage was saved due to David bringing his former "clients" to the church.

Evangelistically Speaking

Stephen Tavani runs a ministry called Wow Jam. They invade inner-city neighborhoods across the country with love and good works. The event is a blowout cross between an evangelistic crusade, a rock concert and a county fair. They fix bicycles and skateboards. Free groceries, haircuts, family portraits and health screenings are all part of the program. The music is loud, the band rocks and they preach Jesus. And they do all this after picking up needles and beer cans off the ground before setting up.

Each event ends with a baptism and a day or two of instruction for several hundred converts. Like most evangelistic events, their retention rate wasn't too hot—until Stephen started launching churches. He recruits leadership from among his converts. They may have been gang leaders or drug dealers—he just looks for people with existing followers.

Gathering these new "pastors," Stephen gives them a crash course in how to operate a simple church built around food, fellowship, worship, an open discussion of Scripture and prayer.

This idea of launching churches is new and still small. But, the new churches are surviving. There are problems, to be sure. But before hitting on this idea the retention rate was horrible. Existing churches always support the outreaches, but they never seem to assimilate people from these hard neighborhoods. It takes someone from the culture to speak into it. Is this the best way to evangelize the inner cities? Probably not. But it does conserve converts, and they'll keep at it until something better comes along. There never is a perfect way to do anything—half the battle is won by showing up!

It's pretty scary to appoint elders from among such young converts in such a pagan world—almost as frightening as Paul appointing elders in Lystra (you can read the story in Acts 14). Paul had little success in Lystra. He preached, healed a man, and then had to fight off the people who wanted to worship him and Barnabas. Then outsiders stirred the town against the apostles. They stoned Paul until they thought him dead. A few days later, he sneaked back into the city, appointing elders from what had to be a mere handful of new converts. Unconventional? Yes, but also sensible.

The Up-and-Out

I could go on about the house church in a very expensive Honolulu neighborhood that reaches people who feel more comfortable worshiping with their rich neighbors than in our middle-class congregation.

Or how about the guy who searches out church leaders in rapidly growing immigrant populations? He simply befriends these people who are newly adapting to their communities, aids them with adjusting to their new culture, and points them toward planting churches among their own people. Not all of them have green cards, either.

I could tell you about the prison ministry in Las Vegas that enjoys rapid growth by appointing "pastors" among the inmates. There is an effort to obtain denominational credentials for these imprisoned ministers of God's grace.

Talk about invading Satan's kingdom is cheap. Actually doing it requires imagination, vision and a little courage. If you're still reading, you probably possess those qualities.

A Brain Game

So what would a new church look like? Try a little brain game. Get three innovative people together. Read Acts 16. Then read the letter to the Philippians. Ask yourselves, "What did this church look like when Paul met with them upon release from prison?" "Who would have led the church?" "Where did they meet?" "What would they have done in their meetings?" "How did they become so generous?" Turn your answers into kind of a training manual for whatever church multiplication will look like in your situation.

The Church Multiplication Zoo

My friends in the house-church movement like to talk about rabbits and elephants. What most of us deem "house church" is too limiting a term. This powerful movement rightly prefers the term "simple church" because their small congregations meet in all sorts of locations.

Simple churches are capable of rapid multiplication—like rabbits. What they call "legacy churches" (the rest of us) multiply like elephants—quite slowly, if at all. This is a good observation. Ask yourself a question, "Which animal carries the most meat?" Obviously the elephant wins that quiz. Then ask another question, "If I had to feed an army, would I raise elephants or rabbits?" You get the picture.

But I don't think the choice is between planting elephants or rabbits. A better answer is to plant both. Actually, if you take seriously the examples I wrote about earlier in this chapter, we should plant churches that look like a zoo. Our world is a potpourri of cultures, so why not adjust to it?

Why not admit that our building-centric, education-heavy model won't win the world, and then get on with something that looks a lot more like church in the days of the apostles? Two-thirds of the people on this planet will die without knowing Christ. Winds of change sweep across Western minds, undermining our ability to change that fact. We live in a time of struggle in the traditional strongholds of the gospel. It's time that we took a strategic look at the way we've been waging spiritual war. The gates of hell tremble in Nepal, China and Nigeria. Why not make that the case where you live?

• •

Another invitation: On my blogsite, I regularly post short video testimonies of churches that color outside of the lines. You can watch these at www.ralphmoorehawaii.com. Just look for the links section on the front page of the site.

21

EQUIPPING

· · · · · · · · · · · · · · · · · · · ·

HOW TO READY YOUR
CHURCH TO MULTIPLY

The best way to make haste is very slowly. The year 1942 taught us that. America had to be taught the need before engaging in a costly war.

A generation of Americans returned from the First World War intent on avoiding another war at any cost. President Roosevelt and other leaders spent many precious days preparing Americans for the fight. All the while, Hitler and Tojo cut down European and Asian armies like spring grass.

American thinking had to change or else its industrial prowess would remain useless. Evil would triumph in Europe and Asia. Franklin Roosevelt displayed the patience of a preschool teacher as he coaxed millions of citizens to care about events far from their shores. He carefully taught this nation the real risks it faced. He advanced us into readiness for war the way a short yardage passer moves his team within sight of the end zone.

When war finally arrived, we were ready to pay the price for freedom. Our president had managed to expand our vision enough to bend our peace paradigm into a tool for fighting aggression. It was only after plowing the ground of public opinion that the great industrial abilities coupled with an indomitable spirit could bear down on the "European problem."

Changing paradigms requires time and teaching. If we would multiply the church we must first change some of our most intuitional opinions. Bigger is not always better. Gathering is not the same as sowing. Comfortable Christianity only works when persecution remains at bay.

We must teach multiplication values before implementing multiplication strategies. These are the values of the kingdom of God. A seed must fall into the ground and die before bearing fruit. It doesn't *feel* right, but it *is* right. It is, after all, better to give than to receive. You *do* multiply by dividing, and you subtract by merging. Anti-intuitive, but also true.

These concepts must take hold in any congregation that chooses to multiply in a healthy manner. Fail to change the paradigm and a church multiplication experiment becomes a one-time flop.

Teach While You Preach

During my first year of pastoral ministry, I attended a seminar at one of the great churches in the country. I was the youngest pastor to attend and the earliest into a pastorate—just two weeks into a congregation numbering 19 people. You might say that I was teachable.

I still remember much of what got into my notes during that week. One of those gems seems pretty obvious: "Your people are teachable!" That's it. It's a given, but one that we often overlook. We come to bless, to entertain and to instruct folks toward a better life. But we can also teach them the larger priorities of God's kingdom. They will get it.

Too often, missional teaching is limited to the hardcore members of the church. For the rest, it's for us to know and for them to follow. That may be fine if your goals roughly parallel the thinking of your members. But start talking about giving away large sums of money or hiving off a significant number of your members and you discover that if they aren't for you, they might turn against you.

If you intend to multiply your congregation (more than once), you need to gently leak your intent and the attendant values into your preaching for a year or so. Significant change requires significant time. Dripping water does melt rock. Build the paradigm from the pulpit before you build it into your structures.

OJT: On-the-Job Training

After teaching values, you can look for basic structural changes allowing the smooth rise and education of potential pastors from within your local church. What do you teach regarding mission? Is church multiplication a function of your recognized vision? If so, do your structural forms support that function?

Does your church culture suggest organic movement all the way from being a convert to being a pastor? Do you rely heavily on outside training events and institutions, or have you built an organization capable of coaching people to the next level from within? Do you believe in disciplemaking as a viable tool to prepare someone for pastoral ministry? Do you understand the power of on-the-job training?

Let's look at a few examples of on-the-job training. Then we'll superimpose them on a church.

Surfing is Hawaii's gift to the world. Whenever I travel, I encounter people interested in surfing. If they are surfers they want to know if I know the best spots. If they are nonsurfers, they usually ask me if I've ever ridden 30-foot surf at Aimee Bay. Of course, I disappoint them.

They see the pictures, and it all looks so easy. Yet the pictures and the films can't possibly show the endless hours of paddling and practice that produce great surfing ability. Surfers continually experiment with their moves and abilities. They learn by doing. The same holds for ministry. We learn ministry best by doing ministry.

Few people have learned to surf by simply paddling out into the water and trying to learn. Meaningful practice usually involves a coach. You can't learn surfing by reading books. You can learn *about* the sport, but you'll never really know what to do unless someone takes time to teach you. The best method is to get in the water and imitate your teacher while he or she corrects your mistakes and offers encouragement.

Pilots and surgeons are equipped through hands-on training. They learn their skills in the same way that surfers do. The skilled person works alongside of his disciple. The process is relational and hands-on. It usually requires prodigious amounts of reading in between. But the learning core is hands-on behavior with a coach close by. Because of the informality of the coaching process, we can overlook the fact that it is instructional. In fact, it is the richest instructional environment. Educators lament poor pupil-to-teacher ratios. The classroom is *most effective* when tied into a coaching relationship.

This concept is biblical. Elijah modeled ministry for Elisha. The older man mentored the younger while he practiced his skill and learned to hear the voice of God. Jesus allowed His disciples their countless mistakes, turning them into training opportunities. Paul coached Timothy and others by snail mail. Before that, they worked at his side, learning to imitate all that he did and said. Think about it: the first missionary journey was a recruiting trip to enlist trainable leadership. The New Testament Epistles are a coach's notes to his players.

Follow Me as I Follow . . .

So, you ask, what am I driving at? The answer is simple: a cell-church model. Wait, don't turn me off just yet! I'm not coming at this from a church growth perspective, and I haven't erected a statue to any of the authors of the many books on cell churches. I'm talking about an on-the-job training format that I think I see in the Acts of the Apostles.

Every maturing Christian should have a few followers and a pattern for training them. Disciplemaking is not just for recognized leaders. God holds us all responsible for disciplemaking. Every Christian must produce disciples. "Follow me as I follow Christ" isn't a suggestion. A single mother straining to raise two young children should see them as her disciples. A new Christian who brings a friend into the fold should see that person as his or her disciple. Of course a cell group leader should be a discipler and a disciple at the same time.

Think back to the breakout at Jerusalem. The church exploded with growth in a single day. Thousands of infant Christians met in the temple and from house to house. Just 12 apostles (assuming the validity of Matthias) were available to make sense of it all. Those house meetings approximated what we call cell groups today. Cell groups present a great opportunity to coach someone while he or she coaches others. And there is the sure progression of a Stephen or a Philip into more significant ministry.

Do you have a meaningful structure to sustain on-the-job training for pastoral ministry? You will need one if you intend to multiply your church often.

First Priority: Disciple Your Staff

In our situation, I disciple my staff. We read books in sync, then discuss them in our staff meeting. We pray and minister to each other in the same meeting—it usually lasts a couple of hours on Tuesdays. And that is before we do our business. I think discipling the staff is as important as preparing a message and certainly more important than any day-to-day planning.

The staff, in turn, disciples leaders of our MiniChurches. We either do this by reading books together or by operating as a MiniChurch made up of leaders. The MiniChurch leaders all have apprentice leaders they disciple. Together they disciple the members of their MiniChurch—a dozen people who gather weekly to share what the Spirit has said to them during the weekend sermon, to share life experiences and pray for each other. They also eat lots of sweets!

My point is that the MiniChurch discipleship chain produces nearly all of our staff pastors. Each year it also produces one or two pastors capable of planting a new church. It is all pretty simple. It should look a little different in every congregation. But it is biblical and necessary to a church that wants to multiply on multiple occasions.

Every Leader Has a Follower

Uncle Sam, it seems, is always looking for a few good men and women—at least he is every time I go to the post office. Then again, so are we.

Leadership discovery and development is at the heart of everything we do in church. Granted, I've looked in all the wrong places. As a young pastor, I accepted anyone who said they wanted to "start a ministry," with scary results! I've hired from the outside only to discover that the person could not accommodate our unique church culture. I've run leadership-training seminars only to have half the people drop out and discover that half the graduates weren't interested. Nor were they natural leaders. It is the word "natural" that interests me.

I've found a fail-safe method for discovering natural leaders. Now, give me a break. I know that sounds arrogant, especially when Warren Bennis says you can't even adequately define the term "leader."[1] But my method works.

It came to me many years ago when we were trying to "invent" a cell-group structure in the first church I pastored. A number of us had assembled to hear a consultant help analyze the health of our church. The glaring discovery was that we had no workable plan for discipling people through the process of maturing into ministry.

We were quite young and given to quick moves. In six hours we hatched a plan that has worked well for several decades and has proven infinitely reproducible. Then we decided to spring it on the church less than 24 hours after inventing it—I told you we were young and impetuous.

Between Saturday evening and Sunday afternoon, we telephoned or buttonholed 150 identifiable leaders out of a congregation of just over 600 people. To do so we first had to identify all those leaders. We might have been young but we were wise enough to understand that leadership went beyond the *positional* roles we assign people in a congregation. We asked ourselves several questions: "Who are the natural leaders?" "Who are the rebellious leaders?" "Who are the unacknowledged leaders?"

We made several discoveries. First, rebellious leaders are often good people who simply don't understand, or buy into, our vision. They may push back against our great ideas, but they remain leaders, whether we like it or not. We learned that a 12-year-old girl is a leader if she has two friends who follow her like a wake follows a boat. We learned that every leader can have a meaningful place in our church if we will work to disciple them.

Mostly, though, we learned that "every leader has a follower." Profound, huh? Bet it makes you want a refund on this book. But think about it for a minute. The *fail-safe* identifier of leadership is the presence of a follower.

It doesn't matter what class you took or what book you read; if you don't have at least one follower, you are not a leader. Conversely, if you or I see that a person has a follower, we had better get interested in them, because they are helping (or hurting) us as we lead our church.

How Then Shall We Live?

Some will ask if I am not just a little too cavalier in my approach to pastoral training. I get in trouble from lots of people over this. There are those who think that a three-hour assessment can better predict success than seven years of discipleship. Some worry that the new pastor will preach false doctrine. But that will happen only if they're learning bad stuff from me. There are those who think that our process is too simple—the leaders won't last. But ours do—for decades. Some believe that more cost equals better results, so they hold out for seminary. But seminary cuts out the 40-year-old successful lawyer with a wife, three kids and a tall mortgage.

Then there is the idea of "apostolic succession." No kidding! I came under attack at a convention where I taught because we are creating "self-appointed" pastors without regard to apostolic succession. I simply have no answer to that one—you can't please all the people all the time.

It's pretty simple. If you want to multiply your church, you need some very practical tools in place: (1) sermons that support the sacrifices necessary to do the job; (2) a training module that moves the right person from conversion to planting a church; and (3) the ability to appreciate leaders, not for your investment in them, but for God's gifting at birth. Join these three elements in a culturally appropriate way and you can change the future history of the world.

22

COSTS

· ·

MULTIPLICATION WHEN
RESOURCES ARE LIMITED

Money is nice. Actually, lots of money is nicer. But is it really necessary to the Great Commission? If you believe Jesus, it is not. He said, "Don't take along any money, or a traveler's bag, or even an extra pair of sandals" (Luke 10:4).

Jesus gave pretty much the same instructions to the Twelve as He did to the 72. They were to go proclaim the gospel and, by implication, plant the church. He said they could do it without money, luggage or even an extra pair of shoes.

Ed Stetzer, of LifeWay Research, recently told me that his research shows no correlation between cash investment and the survival rate of new churches. It does show a strong tie between ongoing coaching and the success of newly planted churches. This thing is more about relationships than resources.

I'm not preaching poverty. I wrote an entire chapter about where you can obtain start-up monies in my previous book *Starting a New Church*.[1] But I do want to destroy the argument that says, "We can't multiply our church because we lack the resources." The same goes for resources other than money. We launched our church on a beach. We had great financial backing, but the locals viewed us as outsiders and no one would rent us space for services. We discovered that sound equipment, a huge worship band or a cadre of trained leaders are nice to have but not necessary to multiply the church.

God and Innovation

If we assume that God is honest, then we must assume that He is supplying all our needs at any given time, as He said He would.

That assumption can breed innovation. Think this way: "If I don't have conventional resources, God must be providing what I need in a way that I can't yet see." Problem one is my ignorance of His provision. Toss a little faith into the mix and I am left with a question: "How can we do what must be done with what is in our hands?"

The answer to that question will take a million different forms. But opportunities begin to appear the moment we start believing that God is an adequate supplier.

Take the case of our starting church on a beach with no legal permit and a cop cruising us with suspicious eyes each week just before we took the offering. We innovated to the point of assigning a team of three men to stall the policeman if he got out of his car (we really did want to take that offering and end the meeting without embarrassment).

But how cool is it to be able to say that you started your church under a tree with a suspicious policeman in the mix, all because of a bunch of hard-hearted landlords? The story is just bizarre enough to inspire our people through whatever hard times come our way.

Dare I say it? Today's impossibility is tomorrow's marketing tool if you play it right.

The point is that the lack of resources is actually an opportunity if you peel enough layers off the onion. By the way, our church became famous in our community by word-of-mouth within seven days of our first service under that tree. Lots of people were in the market for an unconventional church.

Prospering with Limited Resources

So how *can* we multiply churches when resources are limited? I think the answer is found in churches that start in homes. And, this is new to me. We've mostly launched new churches by hiving off "chunks" of our congregation. If a person was moving across water, they had to be able to recruit at least a dozen friends before we would work with them (remember, we define leadership around the presence of followers). If they started closer to home, they took the people they had most influenced during their years in our church. On at least four occasions, that has amounted to 20-plus percent of our church.

Today we take a different approach. Rather than pull together an instant crowd, we ask a leader to gather a few fired-up friends and start in a home. There is very little overhead, so money is never an issue. The goal is to coalesce a group with a heart for evangelism and grow from there.

If they never outgrow the home, little harm is done. A healthy church in a home is a success. If they long for the comfort of a larger congregation, they can simply integrate into the life of our church. Reintegration is nothing new for us. Nearly half of those we "chunked off" in the past would return to our congregation. And, sadly, there were always a few who would migrate to another church because ours didn't fit with the newly planted church and they felt embarrassed about it.

Harvard Square

Most will outgrow the home and face the ever-increasing need for a greater resource base. You might ask, "What does a new church need most at this crucial point in its history?" Coaching! They need good coaching to negotiate the considerable pitfalls they will face.

A few years ago, I met with a pastor from Seattle, and his disciple, who felt called to multiply their church by planting a congregation in greater Boston. I brought a friend from Massachusetts to the meeting. The Seattle guys asked two questions, "Where should we locate the church?" and "What is the single most important thing we can give the new pastor?" My friend immediately answered the first question, "Harvaaad, we need a church in Harvaaad Square. The school is the intellectual center of our nation. Start there if you want to do the most good." They bit on that, which left us with the second question. I surprised the older man with my answer, "Just give him yourself."

Harvard Square is a pretty daunting place to plant a church, especially if most everyone who loves you is 3,000 miles away. I advised that pastor to travel to Cambridge at least three times the first year. He needed to hear all the complaints and victories. It was up to him to bring the perspective of his experience to the problems of a fledgling congregation pastored by his very able disciple.

His influence would be particularly important in the area of financial and leadership resources. The resources issues can so easily lead to discouragement, but they have a way of working out if they don't overwhelm you. Actually, I believe this is spiritual warfare and that one of the weapons God gives us is the encouragement of a mentor.

But the mentor had better show up. And show up, he did. A handful of people moved from Washington State to the Boston area. Most got jobs quickly. They soon fizzled on the idea of planting a church at Harvard. But the discipler showed up when his disciple needed him. He coached him back on track, and today a healthy congregation is steadily evangelizing and growing in rented quarters in Harvard Square.

These guys picked some of the rockiest soil in the nation. It will probably never be a megachurch, but it has mega-consequences, partly because they possess the will to multiply. And they are bringing some of the best and brightest lights in our nation to faith in Jesus Christ. Some will have applied to Harvard not knowing they would end up Christians, even potential pastors.

What about multiplying a church with limited resources? The logic is pretty straightforward. You raise pastoral leadership through discipleship in a local church—no cost. The pastor is bi-vocational during the early years. Again no cost at the beginning, and very manageable if the church grows out of the house and must pay their pastor. Space to hold services is much easier to come by through the networking of a small, thriving fellowship than by the effort of a team of people entirely new to a community. The only absolute necessities are a disciplemaking disciple of a dedicated coach and a handful of disciples. The rest will follow naturally.

This is not new or all that radical. Just read Luke and Acts.

Out of Africa

A couple of years ago, I met a guy from Nigeria who gave me a lift to Dulles Airport in D.C. Along the way, I tried to share the gospel with him. As we talked, it came out that I am a pastor and that I had read C. Peter Wagner's encouraging book *Out of Africa,* about the growth of Christianity in Nigeria. The cabbie told me, "Pastor, I must confess that I, too, am a pastor." He explained, "I am actually a missionary sent (from the largest church in Nigeria) to plant a church in your nation's capital."

It turns out that he and his family moved to the United States with no financial support. He started driving a cab six days each week. He began a Bible study in his apartment and moved it into the basement of a mainline church building on Sunday nights when they outgrew the apartment.

When we spoke, he was down to two days a week driving the taxi. His plan was to leave the taxi business six months after we spoke. The congregation numbered more than 150 multi-ethnic adults (more are Caucasians than Africans). They rented a floor in a small office building because the church kept upping their rent as they grew—an irritation that turned into an opportunity. Did I mention that he is one of nearly 200 missionaries sent from his church to major cities in the eastern United States? They all follow pretty much the same model.

Suburban Hawaii, Even Japan

We are seeing success with this model in Oahu. It works for us with young gangsters in the urban core. We have two house churches involving street gangsters who would never attend our suburban middle-class church. Two of our members pastor Friday night churches in their neighborhoods.

The model easily crosses cultures and oceans. One of our smaller Japanese language churches has multiplied new house churches in Honolulu, and they've launched a movement that has managed to double in number annually for the past three years.

Some will remain in houses. And that is a good thing. They are in the best position to multiply rapidly as long as they maintain vision and momentum. A few will inevitably fail; but anyone with experience has a couple of war stories about extremely well-funded failures.

Different Strokes for Different Folks

I completely support the house-church movement in all but one point. I love all the chaos erupting from the life they bring. They are asking some pretty basic questions: "What do you call it? House church, simple church, organic church, or what?" "What do you do with the money when people tithe and you have low overhead?" "How do you keep a rapidly expanding, ever-morphing movement tied together without imposing denominationalism?"

These people are good for us and may well pave the road to the future of the church in the West. But I do part from them on one point. Many see the rest of us as what they call "legacy churches." For some, legacy churches translate to outmoded elephants doomed to extinction because of inability to reproduce and an ever-increasing appetite for money and other resources.

It is here that I beg to differ. I say, different strokes for different folks. There will always be families looking for a bigger fire to warm the hands of their junior high kids. Legacy churches meet needs that easily go untended in smaller groups.

We are trying to launch house churches that will remain house churches until Jesus comes. The reason is that rabbits do multiply faster than elephants. But if a small congregation feels a need to rent ever-larger quarters and grow far larger than our church, I will only applaud them and coach the pastor along the way.

We have come to the house as *the* place to start. From there we can go in any direction. We support both the rapid multiplication of rabbit churches or the slower growth and reproduction of elephants. We want to be an "and" church, not an "or" group.

Strategic Spending of Limited Resources

That last paragraph brings me to a final thought. What do you do if you are part of a denomination and they supply funds for multiplying your church? I still think you incubate a church in a home. If it remains in the home, leave the money for someone else to spend. If the church outgrows the home, front-load the spending to draw a crowd and let that crowd fund the day-to-day needs of the church.

Whatever you do, do not spend church multiplication money on a pastor's salary if you can help it. Don't rent office space when an electronic "virtual office" can get the job done. Save the money to make a splash.

Think about money this way: God is the ultimate supplier. If we depend on denominational support it will never be enough, no matter how large the sum—that's the nature of human nature. In fact, some have observed that the bigger the check and the longer it is paid the more helpless and dependent the new church. If you depend on God, the funds are limitless. But you have to believe that He is and that He is a rewarder of them that diligently seek Him (see Heb. 11:6).

23

MOMENTUM

· ·

MANAGING THAT MOST IMPORTANT MANAGEMENT FACTOR

Managing resources is a crucial component in any successful operation. Think again to the European war. At the beginning, we had few soldiers, and they were pitifully supplied. Every jeep and airplane had to count. In those early months the military actually ferried aircraft back and forth between Europe and the Pacific, depending on the need. They needed to maintain momentum wherever they had it. Much the same happens within the spiritual war we wage. We must marshal resources to maintain momentum.

I love to plant new churches. I've had the privilege of participating directly in the birth of more than 60 new churches over the past 30 years. The secondary church plants (granddaughter and great-granddaughter churches) are more than 12 times that number. But, I am still learning about how to improve the process.

Most of our churches came to life by hiving off people, money and leaders from the mother church. That is by far the *easiest* way for us to plant a new congregation. It also guarantees a measure of success. Over the life of my pastoral tenure, we have on four different occasions given away an excess of 20 percent of our members to a new congregation. God has always replaced the people, and the mother church has never yet regretted a birth.

Thinking Differently

Recent events have changed the way I think about church planting. They are causing me to rethink our model. The trigger point was a comment my wife made over breakfast. I was complaining that we were having a difficult time bouncing back from our most recent church plant. Finally, I concluded that it was really the past five plants that took the wind out of our sails. We weren't growing any larger—just regaining our numbers after planting a new congregation each autumn.

Four Costs of Planting Churches

My observant wife said that it is because you lose not three (as I always say) but four ingredients each time you plant a church. "You lose people, cash flow, part of the leadership base and *passion*." She went on to say, "The most passionate people are usually the newest converts—their passion drives them to want to help plant a new church. The transfer members always stay with you. You are gradually turning our congregation into a church of dispassionate transplants and long-term Christians who have lost some of the fire of their faith."

I couldn't help my sometimes-chauvinistic self. I had to admit that she was right. We bleed passion every time we plant a new church. And it doesn't come back all that easily.

When we launch a new church, our attendance statistics usually (though not always) take a brief dip. But within a couple of weeks we are right back where we were before the launch date. The offerings take a little longer to heal; say, until the next of our annual tithing series. Leadership is much slower to develop. Once, we started a large congregation with most of the young urban professionals in our church. It was four years before we healed the leadership deficit they left behind.

Leaking Away Passion

What about passion? I hadn't considered the possibility that we ever lost any. In fact, we usually make such a big deal about the birth of a baby church that you might think we were more passionate in the aftermath. But we aren't—at least not this year.

Passion is an odd thing. It is hard to conjure. Seems to be more a work of the Spirit in the life of a believer. And it is true that new Christians possess more of it than veterans and certainly more than those who joined our church because they were burned out somewhere else. Passion is a precious commodity.

My original comments about not bouncing back were evidence of a lack of passion. In the early days, we would give away a huge crowd and still see net numerical growth at the end of the year. That is because, as a young church, we were still brimming over with passion, and most of our members were first-generation Christians.

That is no longer true. We've planted so many churches that we have sifted a lot of passion right out of our midst.

So what do we do? We don't want to quit planting churches. We believe it is part of the New Testament mandate. It is the primary way the apostles approximated delivery on the great commission. Our task is simply to find a more efficient way to do the job. We must build a method that protects passion while it continues to rapidly launch new churches.

Lowering the Cost of Planting Churches

So how can we cut some of these costs? I am especially interested in dealing with the drain in the area of passion. Without it we are dead in the water. I am not interested in pastoring a church in maintenance mode, even if it pops out a new congregation each year. Our problem is that for several years we have multiplied our congregation by one or two churches per year, but we only grow enough to replenish our numbers before we do it again. We think we need to lower the cost of planting new churches.

A Bit of Friendly Advice

I brought up these concerns to a circle of seasoned church planters I met with recently. I had the privilege of hosting a meeting of pastors who had not only planted the churches they pastor, but they had also launched multiple congregations during their tenure.

In that meeting, I discovered a paradigm that I had not only overlooked, but I had also disdained over the years. Most of these churches limit the number of people they allow a planter to take with them. This was news to me. I guess I am still a 1970s hippy at heart. The idea of limiting the size of the team has always smacked of too much "establishment control" over the process.

Frankly, I was a bit taken aback when I heard the controls these churches put on the church-planting process. But then I began to think about the controls attendant to the process of human birth. Only two parents are allowed into the process. Furthermore, the hospital severely limits the number of people in the birth room. Thinking that allowed me to accept the limitations that my friends put on the process of birthing churches.

Limiting the Number of People You Send
Each of these pastors had a different formula for the number of people they send on a church-planting team. The numbers

ranged from a handful to 50. The middle ground of 20 to 30 was most common. This is in stark contrast to the generosity that has ruled our congregations for the past 31 years. Four times we've given away 20 percent of our congregation. The number crept up to 25 percent when we planted two churches on the same day.

What struck me about these pastors was their determination to control numbers in order to protect the mother church. They likened the loss of too many people to the loss of blood a new mother can face while bringing a newborn into the world. Each of them set a quota on the number of people a planter could recruit from the mother church. Most of them asked the planter to show them a regularly updated list of whom they were recruiting. All of this was necessary if the planter wanted the blessing and financial support of the mother church.

Limiting the Loss of Leadership

Overall numbers are one thing. The loss of key leaders is another. One church planter I know intentionally targeted the strongest lay leaders in the church that sponsored him. He was almost haughty in his approach. Of course, he showed great disdain for the church that brought him to Christ. The pastors I spoke with simply would not allow that to happen.

With their lists, they could regulate the mix of who goes out to the new church. They require planters to recruit a wide mix of leaders, followers and new Christians. They actually discuss who will be invited before the invitation is made. They make trade-offs. "You can take this one if you leave me that one . . ." It sounds like the NFL draft, but it works.

Limiting a Financial Burden

It costs money to fund new churches. Mother churches invest money in two ways. They give away the money they budget to directly invest in the project. They *also* give money in the form of the tithers they send along with the new pastor. This is a hidden cost. It is also, by far, the larger cost.

Again, the pastors I met with limit this cost. First, by limiting the overall number of folks who leave the church, they constrain the cost to the mother. But they also negotiate the number of strong givers who will be invited into the project. One man told me that he found a mature staffer poring over the tithe records of his church. The guy was building a list of the strongest donors in the church. That would have been his recruitment list if he hadn't been caught. The parent church pastor not only made him destroy the list, but he also held him back from planting until his character caught up with his calling.

Limiting Your Loss of Passion

The most passionate people in any church are usually found in the ranks of the intensely involved and of the newest converts. The intensely involved are usually leaders, so manipulating team lists obviously covers them.

New converts are something else. No one can know how they will fare as leaders or givers until they've been around a while. In some cases, a planting pastor wouldn't even know them because they are so new in the church. How do you recruit them? Or how do you recruit them with any sense of strategy? The pastors I talked with said they encouraged church planters to leave the gleaning of new converts for public announcements.

This strategy calls for a blitz of the mother church two weeks before the church-planting team leaves. At this point, anyone who wants to join them can do so. Many who do will be those new Christians who are brimming with passion.

Leaving them out of the process until the last minute guarantees that you don't lose a strong part of the passion base in the parent church.

In other words, don't recruit them to the team meetings. Keep that for the people whose performance you can predict.

A Last Thought

Most of the pastors I met with will only allow a planter to recruit people from the parent church if they already have an established relationship with them. In other words, "If you didn't pastor them while you were here, I won't allow you to pastor them elsewhere." Of course this can't apply to those who might come because of a public announcement. But it is good advice. After all, this thing called "church" is above all supposed to be about relationships.

Looking back to the meeting and my thoughts going in, I know I learned a lot that day. I learned that you can keep things more relational by being a little bit more institutional. I also learned some great strategies for limiting the losses we take when multiplying our congregation.

PART 6

STAND AND DELIVER

24

EXPECTATIONS

. . . .

COULD OUR CONGREGATION SPAWN A MOVEMENT?

My wife and I started a church with 12 people way back in 1971. Fortunately, it happened at a time of great upheaval in America—which made it easier to experiment with new ideas. The sexual revolution was upon us. Universities openly bristled with drugs for the first time. Our cities ruptured over racial issues and conflicted feelings over an unpopular war in Southeast Asia.

As a generation of high school students, we were influenced to question authority. By the time we hit college, the fruit of that influence permeated the culture. In those days, "overwhelming" authority was the preoccupation of student America. The country would never be the same after the late 1960s and early 1970s. A few years into the revolution, a handful of friends joined my wife and me to launch a church. We were primed for rapid change. Our church would certainly be different from the one that birthed it.

On top of our devotion to change, the Holy Spirit interfered. Two strangers, on two different occasions, "prophesied" that our church was going to be different from anything we had known—so different that we shouldn't bother to pray about it. We were just to expect something different. Not given to personal prophecy, I ignored the first "word." But when another person said exactly the same thing to me in an entirely different location three months later, I took notice. But that is all I did.

The Birth of Hope Chapel

The "new thing" happened as we launched a church plant from our fledgling congregation. If this story sounds familiar, it is—I described another aspect of it in chapter 20. The new church met in a home. The pastor was bi-vocational, and he had no formal training. The lack of education was a big log for me to crawl over. In fact, when the group first broached the idea, I flatly refused to support it. I only became convinced of the possibility after the Navigators recruited the potential pastor to serve as a missionary in another country. If they believed in him, why shouldn't I?

Aside from the narrow channel of my mind, the other obstacles were denominational. Our group had a rule against two churches in one city, and there were already two of them resenting one another for breaking the rule. Adding a third could only cause more conflict.

Our denominational bylaws *required* formal education for pastors. This guy had no "credentials," so we had to pull a rabbit out of a baseball cap to pull off a new church. No formal credentials, maybe, but he did bring impressive assets to the project. He was *successfully* leading five Bible studies each week besides heading a strong family and running his own business. The issues of salary and building were no problem. He earned good money in finish carpentry on upscale homes. The group met in a house so they didn't need a building. Besides that, they had a line on an empty space they could rent if the new congregation grew—it was a bar. Finally, the rookie pastor and

I had a strong relationship; we were so close that you would be hard-pressed to discern who was discipling who.

Anticipating institutional reticence, we decided to go with that wonderful proverb, "It's easier to gain forgiveness than permission!" We started the church and then informed the denomination. To our surprise, they embraced the baby church like parents who overcome skepticism about their kid's marriage at the sight of their first grandchild. They even paraded us before several thousand people at their convention to tell how a local church had birthed a congregation—something that hadn't happened in decades.

Our church was called Hope Chapel. The new congregation dubbed itself "a Branch of Hope." I balked. I wanted them to remove the word "hope" from their name. I feared criticism for starting a denomination within a denomination. They kept the name.

Within weeks, a second congregation spontaneously unfolded among a number of newly saved Jewish-American students at Santa Monica City College. We'd become a movement in incubation—almost without choice. Those "prophecies" were coming to fruition. We had stumbled into something so new that we couldn't have imagined it. We, quite literally, would not have known how to pray for it because we had no vision for it.

Out of Control Multiplication

Now, many miles down the road, I've still only personally started one youth group, planted two churches and had a direct hand in multiplying just over 70 church plants from the congregations that I pastored. Somewhere along the way, the multiplication process got out of control. Those few churches have become a *movement* that keeps generating new congregations.

To date we can identify more than 700 church plants. Each is a direct relational outgrowth of that original 12 people in a Southern California beach town. (We do not count churches where we simply encouraged another group to begin multiplying churches. These are direct descendants.)

In New England, we can identify growth that runs through nine generations of pastors each taking the baton from one leader almost simultaneously and passing it on to the next. We plant churches in Japan. And one man launched over 100 churches in Pakistan while being discipled long-distance by a businessman in our church. A young convert got the bug for church multiplication in our first couple of years. When I bumped into him years later, I discovered that he pastors a large church in South America and has multiplied more churches than the rest of our "movement." The thing is out of control—and that is exactly as it should be.

We don't govern churches. We've birthed congregations in a maze of denominations. Many are in our own church family, but most are independent congregations. In countries where persecution is an issue, some have banded together corporately in order to gain government protection.

This is all so loose that we can only approximate the number of churches. Even then we only attempt to tally numbers about every four years. We simply contact all the known churches in the network, asking, "Have you planted any new churches since we last spoke?" We get contact info for the newest churches and call them with the same question. As you can imagine, this has become a ponderous task. We last polled growth three years ago and are uncertain as to whether to even attempt it in the future. The only reason we ever counted in the first place was to force church multiplication onto other people's agenda in an era that saw megachurches as the answer to the world's problems. Besides that, keeping count has helped us maintain a priority within the movement toward ongoing multiplication of churches.

The Chaotic Nature of Growth

I used to feel pretty uneasy about the chaotic nature of what has grown up around the simple idea of multiplying our congregation. Then I read a book called *The Starfish and the Spider*. The subtitle says a lot: *The Unstoppable Power of Leaderless Organizations*. The book describes the unsurprising death of a spider that gets poked in the head with a pin. It contrasts that to the resilience of starfish, which can survive just about anything. Most starfish will grow a new appendage (do you call them legs, arms or points?) if it is cut off. In one species, the severed appendage will grow into a whole new body.[1]

You get it! Each cell of that starfish carries DNA capable of reproducing the whole organism. I think that is how Christ intended His Church. Each member should be capable of reproducing the whole. The Early Church appears to have been a somewhat chaotic, nearly leaderless organization (unless you count Peter as the first pope and the Jerusalem Council as executive officers). But this was the genius of it all. I no longer cringe at the chaos of what has grown from our church. I now relish the extreme flexibility of it all.

My role in all this is pretty simple. My job is to keep an ideal alive. To keep people thinking that the unseen is more important than the seen. That what they could become is far greater than what they've been. That what they might accomplish has more to do with the ability of God to bless something than it does with their experience or their personal abilities. My task, as I see it, is to keep people focused on discipling nations rather than just building churches. My life goal is to stimulate others to plant movements instead of settling for just growing congregations or even planting a few churches.

Movements are dynamic and sloppy. They are alive, not static. Difficult to contain, they prefer pragmatism and innovation to institutions and traditions. They seek to inspire and empower rather than control people. Movements esteem teamwork and ordinary "heroes" above superheroes.

A denomination may be a movement, but usually is not. Similarly, gathering a bunch of pastors around a heroic leader may be useful, but a movement it is not. A movement procreates relationally through simple, easily reproducible models and systems. A movement sustains itself through multiple generations geographically as well as historically.

A Helpful History Reminder

The Holy Spirit blesses movements. While the Twelve held council in Jerusalem, a bunch of unnamed people launched churches in Cyprus, Cyrene and eventually in Antioch. From Antioch the Spirit kicked off a church multiplication movement that would sketch the history of Europe and the Mediterranean.

After Rome fell, a young Englishman held slave to Irish tribesmen broke captivity when Jesus informed him of an escape route in a dream. Back home he converted to Christianity only to sense a call to carry the gospel to his former captors. Years later, Patrick traveled across Ireland, healing the sick and preaching God's kingdom as he made transit to the village of his former misery. From there, he discipled a nation.

A generation later, the Irish monk Columba launched a pitiful little boat load of 12 "brothers" into the Irish Sea with no particular destination in mind. They had a goal, but no destination. Once they reached deep water, they jettisoned oars and sail, trusting the Holy Spirit to take them wherever He could best use them. The sea could have swallowed them. It didn't. They could have died of dehydration in the middle of the North Atlantic. But they survived. Rocks as sharp as razor blades could have flayed them like Atlantic Cod. Instead they fell ashore on a rare sandy beach on the coast of Scotland. After evangelizing that nation, those motivated priests launched underground missionary raids, preaching and planting churches across the then post-Roman, post-Christian European continent.[2]

As movements go, the Protestant Reformation comes to mind, as does Puritanism in England and the American Colonies. In turn, England and the United States simultaneously birthed the great evangelical movement that we still identify with the worldwide growth of Christianity.

The underground church in China is busy launching their "army of worms" and sending secret missionaries into Muslim lands. The Christians in Nigeria have missionaries strategically placed in the post-Christian industrial nations of Eastern and Western Europe, and even Japan and the United States. As I write, the church grows faster in Mongolia and Nepal than in most other nations.[3] The Holy Spirit indeed specializes in movements.

So, What About Your Church?

The sum of all of our goals will fall short of discipling nations. By that, I mean, if you could gather the strategic plans of every congregation, every spontaneous movement, even every denomination, the total of all their goals would fall short of total saturation evangelism.

Bummer! We should think bigger. We should be more responsible. We should this or that! But we can't. None of us is responsible for eating the whole watermelon of world evangelism. We can, however, reassess our situation. We could take another look at our disciplemaking processes. We could start to raise our sights simply by choosing to turn from leading a congregation toward attempting to lead a cluster of them. If I sound a little simplistic, so be it—simple works. This is ultimately a numbers game. If we all multiplied instead of adding, we would be farther down the road.

Your church as a movement will draw fire. Some will criticize. Others won't get their heads around larger goals. But it could happen—and it should.

25

URGENCY

· ·

WHY TODAY IS PREGNANT
WITH OPPORTUNITY

These are the best of times and they are the worst of times.
With due respect to Charles Dickens, you could probably
say that on any day of any week and be pretty much on target. Most problems are pregnant with opportunity.

We're approaching peak oil, so a lot of people will get
filthy rich on solar energy. The Chinese threaten to lead
the global economy, but to do so they had to open the door
to commerce with the West and will necessarily lighten up
on human rights. You get it. Problems are doorways into
new possibilities.

Take the bad news about church attendance in America.
It's half of what we were told for so many years. After you
get over your depression, you awake to realize that our self-
satisfaction might give way to innovation. As you worked
your way through this book, you probably picked up a couple of good ideas. But, then again, you might be hesitant to
give those ideas a shot for fear of upsetting an authority figure in your life. The good news is that particular authority
figure is either on its way out or has awakened to the spiritual crisis right down the road. Either way, you have an opportunity to make some serious changes.

Here's a for instance. For 24 years, our church broadcast on several Christian radio and TV stations. We knew that mostly believers heard the broadcasts—we even thought of spending the money in ways that might better hook up with pre-followers of Christ. But we never had the nerve to adjust the budget—the Christian media helped fill chairs. Then a bad/good thing happened. We had a falling out with one of the media outlets over a difference in theology. We freaked a little, and then began experimenting with web-based contact with the unchurched in our community. Our website traffic is up by about a thousand percent in less than a year—a very good/bad thing, don't you think?

So . . . church attendance is lower than we thought. The so-called "brights" spend enormous amounts of energy promoting books and blogs pitting science against religion, particularly Christianity. And, heaven help us, those emerging churches are a menace to our orthodoxy. But look on the bright side. God is still on the throne. The New Testament patterns of mission are still valid. And, best of all, you are pretty well positioned to try something new.

The attacks on Christianity are getting us lots of press. When under attack, the gospel usually spreads faster than in times of peaceful devotion. And God always brings messy theological arguments to the fore at points of spiritual renewal. Sounds like good news to me. Even more positive is the thought that all people are made in the image of the Creator. Everyone yearns for God, even the most devoted atheist. Most people would hum along with meaning to those words, "I still haven't found what I'm looking for . . ."

We live in a freaky time. Families hardly talk. Video games, blogs and the news channels threaten to drown out our iPods. Technology has made communication a 24/7 occupation, yet people feel more unconnected than ever. And everybody is looking to connect.

I recently read a particularly nasty email being forwarded as SPAM among our more right-wing brothers and sisters. It called for prayer that God would *remove* Oprah, Bono and New Age apostles leading us down the road to destruction. No kidding, they were asking God to "take these people out." Aside from being murderous, these people are nuts. Point one: Bono is a Catholic, not into the New Age. Point two: the New Age is little different from the Roman world where the gospel found such fertile ground. Oprah's book club constantly tosses opportunity our way for interesting and wholesome spiritual discussion with people on the search for God. To paraphrase a slogan from an old political campaign, "It's about the opportunity, stupid!"

This is the day that the Lord has made, we should rejoice and be glad in it. It is a day for small, highly connective networks of people. It's a day for church in the marketplace. It's a day for praying with not-yet-believers when life threatens to crush them. It's a day for cutting back on church programs and encouraging people to spend time hanging out with their friends—and their friend's friends. It's a day for starting churches in offbeat locations without even calling them churches. In short, it is a day for doing something different. It's a day of great and wonderful opportunity.

D-DAY

• •

WILL YOU STAY ON
THE SIDELINES?

If truth be told, we are fighting for the life of Christianity in the West. It is a fight we must win or we will die of irrelevance by the middle of this century. My question is, *What will you and your congregation do about it?*

When D-Day finally came around, some went looking for excuses not to go to war. There were reports of men shooting themselves in the foot or ankle to avoid the engagement. The opposite emotion was one of relief that a man could finally get into the battle. You and I face a D-Day decision regarding the possibility of multiplying our churches. We can even set the date. It is as easy as sketching out a plan, identifying key leadership and marking a day on a calendar—a goal for birthing a new congregation. Most who do this find that the possibilities don't end with only one new church.

You may already pastor thousands of people. Conversely, you may lead a congregation of 40 souls and drive a school bus to put bread on the table. In either case, you *could* raise your sights if you would.

Such thinking might actually be more difficult for the large church pastor than for the man charged with a small flock. Things are simpler in a small setting—pull together a band of young leaders and fill their heads with vision. It's not that hard. I watched one small-church pastor launch a handful of young men into ministry simply by inviting them to hang out at his house for videos and root beer floats on Friday nights. As trust grew, the boys plunked their questions on the table. Steadily satisfying their curiosity, this pastor made disciples who went on to pastor churches of their own.

If you pastor a large church, you might be tempted to over-complicate the task and may then shrink from attempting it. It is good to remember Henrietta Mears—"Teacher" in the eyes of everyone who knew her. Miss Mears's primary job was Christian Education Director at Hollywood Presbyterian Church in the mid-twentieth century. She also taught a Sunday School class numbering hundreds of university students. But her great legacy grows from her practice of cooking breakfast for a group of no more than eight young men each Saturday morning. Over the decades faces changed while the basic theme remained steady: "My job as a trainer of leaders is to spot the potential of a person. . . . It doesn't matter if he is doing anything now or not. I must see where he is capable of going. Then I encourage him along that line."[1]

Miss Mears's disciples included Bill Bright, who multiplied her model into a little organization called Campus Crusade for Christ. Other disciples launched Gospel Light Press, Forest Home Christian Conference Center, Young Life and a host of other Christian organizations. The essential element here is a committed teacher instilling vision and tools in a handful of ordinary people—pretty much the same thing Jesus did for those three-and-a-half years with His disciples.

Back in 1944, the "D" in D-Day simply stood for "day." It was a way of keeping the actual date secret, as was "H-Hour." For our purposes, you might think of D-Day as the day you *decide* to *do* something about the thoughts that are running around in your brain at this moment.

You can do this. The assignment has little to do with money, size or talent. You could launch a movement by meeting informally with a group of young leaders.

A small clump of trees made the ultimate sacrifice to provide paper for the book you hold in your hands. Their demise pays dividends only if you catch a vision for church multiplication. But we achieve bonanza if you figure out that it is normal for a congregation to look more like the one in Antioch than the one in Jerusalem.

It's your church that I imagine here—a church that grows far outside its walls; a church multiplying intentionally and regularly; a church where discipleship is both relational and curricular; a church that inspires its members to see the world as *their own* mission field; a church that instills vision in church planters to give themselves to the lifelong craft of church multiplication.

Can you see it? For sure it's visible if you look deep into the heart of God. But I bet you can find it locked up deep inside your own heart as well. Search for it diligently, for without vision, people perish.

ENDNOTES

Chapter 1: Why 1943 Was a Very Good Year: A Church Multiplication Metaphor

1. Dwight D. Eisenhower, *Crusade In Europe* (New York: Doubleday and Company, 1948), p. 7.
2. Richard Overy, *Why the Allies Won* (New York: W.W. Norton and Company, 1995), p. 227.
3. Martin Gilbert, *The Second World War: A Complete History* (New York: Henry Holt and Company, 1989), pp. 486-488.
4. Overy, *Why the Allies Won*, p. 137.
5. Robert Goralski, *World War II Almanac 1931-1945* (New York: Bonanza Books, 1981), p. 164.
6. Reggie MacNeal, *The Present Future: Six Tough Questions for the Church* (San Francisco: Jossey Bass, 2003), p. 3.
7. Scott Thumma, Dave Travis and Warren Bird, *Megachurches Today 2005* (Hartford, CT: Hartford Institute For Religion Research, 2005), p. 1.
8. Ed Stetzer, *Planting Missional Churches* (Nashville, TN: Broadman and Holman, 2006), p. 9.
9. Rebecca Barnes and Linda Lowry, "A Special Report: The American Church in Crisis," http://www.namb.net/site/c.9qKILUOzEpH/b.1758213/apps/s/content.asp?ct=235 0673 (accessed May 2009).
10. Alan Hirsch, *The Forgotten Ways* (Grand Rapids, MI: Brazos Press, 2006), p. 76.
11. Leonard Sweet, *Soul Tsunami* (Grand Rapids, MI: Zondervan, 1999), p. 390.
12. Kenneth L. Woodward, "The Changing Face of the Church: How the Explosion of Christianity in Developing Nations Is Transforming the World's Largest Religion," *Newsweek*, December 17, 2007.
13. Patrick Johnstone, *The Church Is Bigger Than You Think* (London: Christian Focus Publications, 1998), p. 110.
14. Philip Jenkins, *The Next Christendom* (Oxford, UK: Oxford University Press, 2002), p. 3.
15. Stephen C. Neill, *A History of Christian Missions* (London: Penguin Books, 1990), p. 421.
16. Justin Long and Jason Mandryk, "The Multicultural Team, Money and the Glory of God," *Momentum*, November/December 2006, vol. 1, no. 8, pp. 49-51.
17. C. Peter Wagner, *Out of Africa* (Ventura, CA: Regal, 2004), p. 14.
18. Norimitsu Onishi, "Korean Missionaries Carrying Word to Hard-to-Sway Places," *The New York Times*, November 1, 2004.
19. David Aikman, *Jesus in Beijing* (Washington, D.C.: Regenery Publishing, Inc., 2003), p. 195.
20. Aikman, *Jesus in Beijing*, p. 285.
21. Ed Stetzer and David Putman, *Breaking the Missional Code* (Nashville, TN: Broadman and Holman Publishers, 2006), p. 67.

Chapter 2: Kingdoms in Conflict: A Spiritual Battle We Dare Not Lose

1. Sebastian Junger, "Enter China, the Giant," *Vanity Fair*, July 2007, p. 138.
2. Christopher Hitchins, *God Is Not Great: How Religion Poisons Everything* (London: Twelve Books, 2007), p. 56.
3. Philip Jenkins, *The Next Christendom* (Oxford, UK: Oxford University Press, 2002), p. 5.

4. Kenneth L. Woodward, "The Changing Face of the Church: How the Explosion of Christianity in Developing Nations Is Transforming the World's Largest Religion," *Newsweek*, December 17, 2007.

5. Ibid.

6. D. James Kennedy, *Evangelism Explosion* (Wheaton, IL: Tyndale House Publishers, 1996), p. 3.

7. Jonathan Riley Smith, *The Crusades: A History* (New Haven, CT: Yale University Press, 2005), pp. 18-22.

8. Hopewell Radebe, "South Africa: Slavery Still Alive and Kicking the World Over," *Business Day*, Johannesburg, South Africa, March 31, 2008.

9. Bono, quoted in Michka Assayas, *Bono: In Conversation with Michka Assayas* (New York: Riverhead Books: 2005), p. 207.

10. George Weigel, *The Final Revolution: The Resistance Church and the Collapse of Communism* (Oxford, UK: Oxford University Press, 1992), p. 166.

11. Serge Schemann, *When the Wall Came Down* (Boston, MA: Houghton Mifflin, 2006), pp. 46-48.

12. Paul Kengor, *God and Ronald Reagan: A Spiritual Life* (New York: Regan Books, 2004), pp. 210-211.

13. Eric Metaxas, *Amazing Grace: William Wilberforce and the Heroic Campaign to End Slavery* (New York: Harper Collins Publishers, 2007), p. 121.

14. Vishal and Ruth Mangalwadi, *The Legacy of William Carey: A Model for the Transformation of a Culture* (Wheaton, IL: Crossway Books, 1999), pp. 82-83.

15. Weigel, *The Final Revolution: The Resistance Church and the Collapse of Communism*, p. 34.

Chapter 4: Hope: Imperfect People Moving in the Right Direction

1. Mark Elkin, "The Closing of the Church Door," *Newsweek*, May 19, 2008.

2. Reggie McNeal, *The Present Future: Six Tough Questions for the Church* (San Francisco: Jossey-Bass, 2003), p. 3.

3. Rebecca Barnes and Linda Lowry, "A Special Report: The American Church in Crisis," http://www.namb.net/site/c.9qKILUOzEpH/b.1758213/apps/s/content.asp?ct=2350673 (accessed May 2009).

4. Tom Clegg and Warren Bird, *Lost in America* (Loveland, CO: Group Publishing, 2001), p. 25.

5. Ed Stetzer, *Planting Missional Churches* (Nashville, TN: Broadman and Holman, 2006), p. 13.

6. Dan Kimball, *The Emerging Church* (Grand Rapids, MI: Zondervan-Emergent, 2003), p. 79.

7. David McCullough, *1776* (New York: Simon and Schuster, 2005), pp. 21,58.

8. Ibid., pp. 81-86.

Chapter 7: Roadblocks: What Stands in Our Way?

1. Acts 19:9. See Ralph Moore, *Friends: The Key to Reaching Generation X* (Ventura, CA: Regal Books, 2001), pp. 91-93.

2. Thom S. Rainer and Eric Geiger, *Simple Church: Returning to God's Process for Making Disciples* (Nashville, TN: B&H Publishing Group, 2006).

3. Steven E. Ambrose, *Eisenhower: Soldier and President* (New York: Simon and Schuster, 1990), p. 139.

Chapter 10: Possibility: Doing What Jesus Did

1. Bede, *A History of the English Church and People* (Middlesex, UK: Penguin Books Ltd., 1972), pp. 87-88.

2. Ramsay MacMullen, *Christianizing the Roman Empire: A.D. 100-400* (New Haven, CT: Yale University Press, 1984), pp. 108-109.

Chapter 12: Methods: What Would Paul Do?

1. From Athanasius, *Against the Heathen*, quoted in Frank C. Darling, *Biblical Healing: Hebrew and Christian Roots* (Boulder, CO: Vista Publications, 1989), pp. 160-161.

Chapter 16: Mission: Reaching People Where They Are

1. Roger Finke and Rodney Starke, *The Churching of America, 1776-2005: Winners and Losers in Our Religious Economy* (New Brunswick, NJ: Rutgers University Press, 2005), pp. 55-57.
2. Ibid., p. 73.

Chapter 17: Education: Learning from America's Past

1. Ralph Moore, *Friends: The Key to Reaching Generation X* (Ventura, CA: Regal Books, 2001), p. 91.
2. Kenneth B. Mulholland, *Adventures in Training the Ministry* (Nutley, NJ: Presbyterian and Reformed Publishing Co., 1976), p. 4.
3. Ibid., p. 8.
4. John Dillenberger and Claude Welch, *Protestant Christianity Interpreted Through Its Development* (New York: Charles Scribner's Sons, 1954), p. 148.
5. Neil Braun, *Laity Mobilized: Reflections on Church Growth in Japan and Other Lands* (Grand Rapids, MI: Wm. B. Eerdmans Publishing Co., 1971), p. 55.
6. Edwin Scott Gaustad, *Historical Atlas of Religion in America* (New York: Harper and Row, 1962), p. 55.
7. Roger Finke and Rodney Starke, *The Churching of America, 1776-2005: Winners and Losers in Our Religious Economy* (New Brunswick, NJ: Rutgers University Press, 2005), p. 77.
8. Otis Cary, "Protestant Missions," *A History of Christianity in Japan,* vol. 2 (Tokyo, Japan: Charles E. Tuttle Company, 1976), pp. 163,296.
9. Ibid., pp. 171,320.

Chapter 21: Equipping: How to Ready Your Church to Multiply

1. Warren Bennis and Burt Nanus, *Leaders: The Strategies for Taking Charge* (New York: Harper and Row, 1985), pp. 5-6.

Chapter 22: Costs: Multiplication When Resources Are Limited

1. Ralph Moore, *Starting a New Church* (Ventura, CA: Regal Books, 2002), pp. 89-97.

Chapter 24: Expectations: Could Our Congregation Spawn a Movement?

1. Ori Brafman and Rod A. Beckstrom, *The Starfish and the Spider: The Unstoppable Power of Leaderless Organizations* (New York: Portfolio/Penguin Group, 2006), p. 35.
2. John Eldridge, *Waking the Dead* (Nashville, TN: Thomas Nelson Inc, 2003), pp. 201-201.
3. Patrick Johnstone and Jason Mandryk, *Operation World: 21st Century Edition* (London: OM Authentic Media, 2005), pp. 451,470.

Chapter 26: D-Day: Will You Stay on the Sidelines?

1. Earl O. Roe, ed., *Dream Big: The Henrietta Mears Story* (Ventura, CA: Regal Books, 1990), p. 204.

FOR MORE INFORMATION

· ·

For more information about
Ralph Moore or Hope Chapel, visit:

www.ralphmoorehawaii.com
or
www.hopechapel.com

ALSO FROM RALPH MOORE

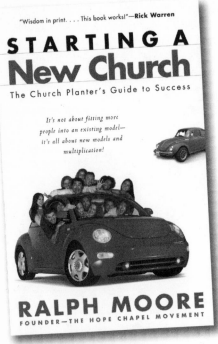

Starting a New Church
Ralph Moore
ISBN 978.08307.29661
ISBN 08307.29666

Rising generations of Americans are ignorant of Jesus Christ and have virtually no moral absolutes. So, who will evangelize them—and what's the best way to go about it? Ralph Moore says the answer is aggressive church planting, but he is also emphatic that established churches can't do the job alone. Why? Because new churches can better meet the needs of each new generation by presenting biblical truth in the cultural context that best reaches those people. *Starting a New Church* will challenge you to consider becoming a church planter, without sugarcoating the problems and practical challenges involved. This book not only covers everything you need to know about starting churches from the ground up, but it also reveals why church planting may be the most dynamic movement in evangelism!